THE
WRIGHT
BROTHERS

AND THE INVENTION
OF THE AERIAL AGE

THE WRIGHT BROTHERS

AND THE INVENTION OF THE AERIAL AGE

TOM D. CROUCH AND PETER L. JAKAB

SMITHSONIAN NATIONAL AIR AND SPACE MUSEUM

NATIONAL GEOGRAPHIC

WASHINGTON, D.C.

It is my belief that flight is possible and,

while I am taking up the investigation for pleasure rather than profit,

I think there is a slight possibility of achieving fame and fortune from it.

WILBUR WRIGHT TO HIS FATHER
September 3, 1900

PRECEDING PAGES | *Elegantly graceful, the Wrights' 1902 glider carries Wilbur above the sands of Kitty Hawk, North Carolina.*

OPPOSITE | *Orville (left) and Wilbur attend an air show in New York in 1910, seven years after their first successful flights.*

Library of Congress Cataloging-in-Publication Data

Crouch, Tom D.
    The Wright brothers and the invention of the aerial age / Tom D. Crouch and Peter L. Jakab.
        p. cm.
    Includes bibliographical references and index.
    ISBN 0-7922-6985-3 (hc.)
    1.Wright, Wilbur, 1867-1912. 2. Wright, Orville, 1871-1948. 3. Aeronautical
engineers—United States—Biography. 4. Aeronautics—United States—History. I Jakab,
Peter L. II Title.

TL540.W7C7824 2003
629.13'0092'273—dc21
[B]

                                                                2002044924

The exhibition "The Wright Brothers and the Invention of the Aerial Age" was made possible through the
generous corporate sponsorship of Alcoa.

CONTENTS

1900

1901

1902

1903

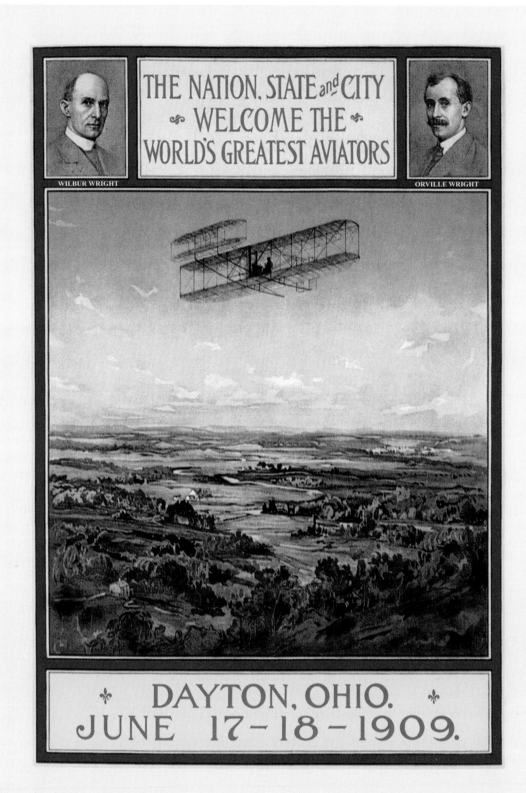

1909: *Home Days Celebration honors Dayton's heroes after their return from a successful tour of Europe.*

PROLOGUE

In the year 1905, at an isolated cow pasture eight miles east of Dayton, Ohio, the world changed. As the hot, sweltering afternoons of summer drifted into the cool, crisp mornings of fall that year, nearby residents and local farmers tending their fields were witnessing with regularity a scene that would become a defining characteristic of 20th-century life: the sight and sound of an airplane flying overhead. Throughout September, a noisy, frail-looking, wood-and-fabric machine frequently circled the hundred-acre meadow known locally as Huffman Prairie. Small groups of friends and family of the birdmen began turning up to see them fly. Even commuters passing by on the interurban railway adjacent to the field were catching glimpses of what appeared to be a huge, white box kite, skimming effortlessly over the cow pasture. For weeks after observing an especially spectacular flight of nearly 40 minutes, on October 5, a three-year-old Dayton boy named Charley Billman raced through his parents' house, arms outstretched, mimicking the sound of the engine. Like the craft that so enthused him, young Charley's playful imitation would become a ubiquitous cultural feature of the 20th century. The age of the airplane had arrived.

The pilots causing passersby to turn their eyes skyward in the autumn of 1905 were, of course, Wilbur and Orville Wright. Although the brothers were drawing more and more spectators as their sustained flights became increasingly routine, their aeronautical work had become quite well known in their hometown even before they were turning circles over the local countryside. The Wrights' regular customers at their bicycle shop for years were vaguely aware of something going on in the back of the shop that had to do with flying machines. And, though filled with wild inaccuracies, the local papers had carried the story of their breakthrough flights at Kitty Hawk on December 17, 1903. Most of the Wrights' neighbors considered their flying experiments rather eccentric, but Wilbur and Orville were still regarded as solid, stable members of the community. When the clattering of their crude engine first began to break the bucolic calm of Huffman Prairie in the spring of 1904, most people simply shrugged it off. The Wright boys' efforts to fly might have been a bit crazy, but they were harmless. So it was during 1904 and 1905 over this untamed patch of Ohio grassland. One of the great technological innovations of the century was ushered in not with spirited public fanfare, but with quiet fascination.

At the close of their 1905 flying season, Wilbur and Orville Wright stood alone in the aeronautical world. After six short years of research and experimentation, they had achieved what countless other would-be aviators had strived for without success. The Wrights had an airplane that could take off under its own power, stay aloft as long as the fuel supply lasted, maneuver precisely through the sky under the full and sure command of the pilot, and land safely to fly again.

The brief flights of the Kitty Hawk airplane two years earlier had proved the Wrights' basic design to be sound. Their third experimental powered machine brought mechanical flight to practicality in 1905. Other experimenters had coaxed ungainly powered aircraft into the air for short, uncontrolled leaps. But none could even remotely claim to have overcome the formidable barriers to heavier-than-air flight. At a time when their peers were still struggling to manage straight-line jaunts measured in feet, the Wrights were consistently covering miles as they circled Huffman Prairie.

It would be three more years before Wilbur and Orville stunned the world with their first major public flying demonstrations in America and Europe in 1908. But the airplanes flown then differed little from the perfected 1905 design. All the fundamental elements of mechanical flight were present in the earlier Wright machine. The aeronautical community quickly caught up to the brothers after 1908. But the building blocks set down by the Wrights in the first years of the new century were the foundation of all airplanes that followed. In every meaningful sense, all successful airplanes incorporate the Wrights' key innovations. Wilbur and Orville had unlocked the door to a new era. Indeed, they had given humans their wings.

IF THE WHEELS OF TIME COULD BE

TURNED BACK SIX YEARS, IT IS NOT

AT ALL PROBABLE THAT WE WOULD

DO AGAIN WHAT WE HAVE DONE....

IT WAS DUE TO PECULIAR

COMBINATIONS OF CIRCUMSTANCES

WHICH MIGHT NEVER

OCCUR AGAIN.

Wilbur Wright

1

THE SEEDS
OF
GENIUS

CIRCA 1900: *Workers pose before the Wright Cycle Company in Dayton, where the brothers built their first successful airplane.*

HY WILBUR AND ORVILLE? HOW DID these two modest small businessmen, working essentially alone, with little formal scientific or technical training, solve a complex and demanding problem that had defied better-known experimenters for centuries? It is perhaps one of the most interesting and important questions that can be asked regarding the invention of the airplane, and the most challenging to answer. Even the Wrights found it difficult to fully explain. Their diaries, letters, notebooks, and photographs revealed much of what they had done, and when. They were far less certain why they had done it, or how they had succeeded where so many others had failed. Wilbur was quick to dismiss the suggestion of his friend and correspondent Octave Chanute, a civil engineer and aeronautical experimenter, that raw genius might be the only explanation. *Do you not insist too strongly upon the single point of mental ability? To me it seems that a thousand other factors, each rather insignificant in itself, in the aggregate influence the event ten times more than mere mental ability or inventiveness.... If the wheels of time could be turned back six years, it is not at all probable that we would do again what we have done.... It was due to peculiar combinations of circumstances which might never occur again.*

Of course, Wilbur knew that "mental ability" lay at the core of the Wright achievement. He was simply pointing to the importance of their background and experiences as factors that had brought them to a point in life where they were able to exercise their extraordinary ability to best advantage. The explanation of why they succeeded begins with another question: Who were Wilbur and Orville Wright?

Wilbur and Orville were quintessential middle Americans, the sons of a pair of extraordinary parents. Most biographers have paid a great deal of attention to the influence of their mother, Susan Catherine Koerner Wright. Born on a small farm near Hillsboro, Virginia, on April 30, 1831, she was the fifth and last child of John and Catherine Koerner. John Gottlieb Koerner had immigrated to the United States from Saxony in 1818, and established himself as a carriagemaker and farmer.

Koerner prospered, and moved his family west to Union County, Indiana, in 1832, where he purchased 170 acres of prime bottomland. In his older years, Orville could still recall the happy hours he had spent as a young boy exploring his Grandfather Koerner's workshop, complete with an array of fascinating tools used in the carriage trade, including a foot-powered lathe.

A painfully, almost pathologically shy person, Susan had grown up in her father's workshop and was gifted with considerable mechanical aptitude. Following her marriage, she built simple household appliances for herself, and made toys for her children, including a sled of which they were especially fond. In contrast, her husband had a difficult time driving a nail straight.

Wilbur and Orville could thank their mother for their lifelong penchant for tinkering, and for their extraordinary gift for visualizing machines that had yet to be constructed. That ability, coupled with their gift for mechanical problem solving, would carry them far.

Susan Koerner was also a well-educated woman for her time and place. Following her graduation from high school, her father sent her to Hartsville College, where she met Milton Wright, a handsome young preacher for the Church of the United Brethren in Christ, who was serving as an instructor in the college preparatory school.

Unlike Susan, Milton came from a family with roots deep in the American soil. The first Wright arrived in Massachusetts in the 1630s. Milton's father, Dan Wright, had moved west with his family in 1814. Milton, born in Rush County, Indiana, on November 17, 1828, grew up as a farm boy. After a religious conversion in 1843, he joined the Church of the United Brethren in Christ in 1847 and became a circuit-riding preacher before taking the job at Hartsville College.

The courtship of Milton and Susan Wright lasted for two and a half years. Shortly after they met, Milton traveled to the Oregon Territory, where he worked as a missionary and helped to establish a new college. He returned home to Indiana in 1859, and married Susan on November 24, 1859. The long separation was to be a forecast of their life together. As he rose through the church ranks from circuit

CIRCA 1900: *A shady porch rims the Wright family home at 7 Hawthorn Street in Dayton. In 1936 Henry Ford bought this house, as well as the bicycle shop, and moved them to his museum complex—Greenfield Village—in Dearborn, Michigan.*

Milton Wright, a minister in the Church of the United Brethren in Christ, and Susan Koerner Wright, shy but well educated, settled their family in Dayton in 1884. Susan bore seven children before dying of tuberculosis in 1889; Milton lived until 1917.

preacher to bishop, Milton would spend extended periods of time away from his family, visiting far-flung Brethren congregations throughout the Middle West and up and down the West Coast of the United States.

Susan accepted her husband's calling as her own. Affectionate and dutiful, she provided Milton with a home, unquestioning loyalty, and absolute support. She bore seven children, the first when she was 29, the last when she was 43. She packed and moved her family 12 times during 30 years of marriage. Most important, she raised their children to become healthy, strong, and self-reliant adults with an extraordinary strength of character to match that of their parents.

The oldest boys, Reuchlin and Lorin, were born in 1861 and 1862. "Reuch" (pronounced Roosh), as he was known in the family, eventually married and established himself on a Kansas farm. After a brief fling tasting life in the "Wild West," Lorin married an old family friend and set up housekeeping in Dayton, Ohio. Lorin's four youngsters (Milton, Leontine, Ivonette, and Horace) were to become great favorites of their aunt Katharine and their uncles Wilbur and Orville.

Wilbur Wright—named for Wilbur Fiske, a fellow clergyman whom Milton admired—was born on a farm near Millville, Indiana, on April 16, 1867. "At fifteen months," Milton would recall many years later, "when turned into a room he seemed to see all of the mischief available in it at a glance, and always found the greatest first."

The young family moved to Dayton, Ohio, in 1869, when Milton took up new duties as editor of the *Religious Telescope*, a church newspaper. Otis and Ida Wright, a twin boy and girl, were born on March 7, 1870, and died soon thereafter. Orville, the next child, was born on August 19, 1871, in an upstairs bedroom of the new family home at 7 Hawthorn Street, across the Miami River on the west side of town. Katharine, the youngest of the Wright children, was born in the same bedroom, three years later to the day.

The family did a good deal of moving around when the children were young. Wilbur, Orville, and Katharine attended schools in Ohio, Indiana, and Iowa. In spite of that, they always regarded Dayton, where they returned to stay in 1884, as home. The precise midpoint of the nation's population in 1870, Dayton was a bustling industrial town that was particularly well known for the manufacture of farm implements and railroad carriages. During the last decade of the 19th century it would emerge as the world center for the production of cash registers and an early leader of the bicycle and automobile industries in America. All in all, it was the perfect hometown for a pair of budding young technicians.

Wilbur and Orville Wright would always credit their parents for much of their success in life. This was a warm, loving, and protective family in which children were encouraged to experiment, think for themselves, and support one another.

The three youngest children grew exceptionally close to one another. Wilbur and Orville, in particular, became inseparable companions. "From the time we were little children," Wilbur once remarked, "my brother Orville and myself lived together, played together, worked together, and in fact, thought together. We usually owned all of our toys in common, talked over our thoughts and aspirations so that nearly everything that was done in our lives has been the result of conversations, suggestions and discussions between us." That close relationship would ultimately become one of the keys to their success.

Bishop Milton Wright is remembered, even today, as the most influential and controversial figure in the history of the Church of the United Brethren in Christ. Traditionally, Freemasons had been barred from membership in the church. Beginning in 1869, a group of young reformers interested in boosting the church's membership began to agitate for the adoption of a more democratic structure and the modernization of traditional rules. Milton, a traditionalist, emerged as a leader of the conservative opposition to change.

The internal struggle for control of the church continued for some 20 years. In 1889, when Wilbur was 22 and Orville 17, Bishop Wright brought matters to a head, creating a national schism in the church that would last for three-quarters of a century. Taking perhaps 10 percent of the total membership with him into a new organization, Milton spent the next ten years battling his old colleagues for the control of church property. The resulting legal cases eventually reached the supreme courts of seven states. Bishop Wright lost every case but one.

Incredibly, just as this decade of crisis was drawing to a close, Milton Wright proceeded to generate an entirely new conflict within the schismatic branch that he had led away from the original church. A resulting set of new court cases (the bishop was a firm believer in litigation) and church disciplinary hearings would continue up to the time of the bishop's retirement in 1905.

Milton Wright believed in the moral absolutes of right and wrong. He was not a man to compromise or negotiate. Once he had made up his mind, he could seldom be moved. He had inherited his unbending character, strength of will, and commitment to principle from his own father, and he passed them on to his children. He taught them that the world was a dangerous place for honest folk. Temptation lured the weak in spirit from the path of virtue. Friends would fall away in times of trial. Family ties offered the best support one could hope for in life.

The lessons of life that Wilbur and Orville Wright learned at their father's knee would serve them well during the difficult years of technical problem solving that led to the invention of the airplane. Ironically, the same lessons would also make it difficult or impossible for them to deal effectively with the different set of problems that they would face as businessmen and public figures during the years after 1905. Their relentless drive and will, their ability to look skeptics and rivals in the eye without

Orville at 9 (left) and Wilbur at 13 were born in 1871 and 1867 respectively. They traced their curiosity about flight to approximately this age, when their father brought home a toy helicopter powered by a rubber band.

1898: *At top, Wilbur pauses during a country outing. At home, the family's Christmas tree brightens the parlor in 1900, and Wilbur and Orville's brother Lorin shows off his children, Milton, Leontine, and Ivonette, a year later.*

The Seeds of Genius

1899: Orville (standing) hosts a party at Hawthorn Street. His guests are looking at a collection of photographs.

Though gregarious, social, and successful, neither Orville nor Wilbur ever married.

Beloved sister Katharine assumed a maternal role when their mother died. Spunky and smart, she graduated from Oberlin University

and taught English and Latin in a Dayton high school.

blinking, their absolute self-confidence—all were a gift from their father. So, too, were their hard-edged and uncompromising personalities, and their fundamental distrust of the world beyond their doorstep.

They grew up in a house that was a psychological fortress and a bastion to which their father could retreat from the bitter struggles with church foes. Within that home, the children found the love, strength, and support that would sustain them in their own struggles with what they literally regarded as the forces of evil and depravity.

It should not come as any great surprise to discover that those children had great difficulty in forging relationships outside the family circle. Neither Wilbur nor Orville would ever marry. Katharine did not marry until the age of 52. Late in his life (he died in 1917) it was Milton's proudest boast that his three youngest surviving children still lived beneath the paternal roof. None of them had found any dearer friends or stauncher supporters than the members of their family.

The events leading up to the invention of the airplane were rooted in a family crisis that began in 1884, the year in which the Wright family moved home to Dayton after several years of living in Iowa and Indiana. The move, necessitated by Milton's preparations for an upcoming church battle, came so quickly that 17-year-old Wilbur, an excellent student, was unable to complete the course work required for his high school graduation.

Rather than wasting his time on mere formalities, the young man enrolled in a series of college preparatory courses at Dayton's Central High School. His plans to enter Yale as a divinity student were shattered when he was struck in the face by a stick during a game of "shinny," a kind of free-form ice hockey. The facial injury was followed by a series of more serious complaints, loosely diagnosed as digestive problems and heart palpitations. Perhaps the young man's physical problems were rooted in an unconscious rejection of adult responsibility in favor of the comfort and security of adolescence. Wilbur was teetering on the brink of becoming that stock character of Victorian family life—the perpetual invalid.

He spent the next three years closeted away at home, sunk in deep depression. The time was not entirely wasted. Wilbur read widely in his father's excellent library; nursed his mother, who was dying of tuberculosis; and kept house for his father, brother, and sister. Friends and family members grew concerned about the sudden transformation of an active and athletic young man into a housebound "cook and chambermaid."

Wilbur emerged from his shell rather abruptly during a period of extraordinary family crisis in the spring and summer of 1889. In May of that year, Milton cut the Gordian knot of a 20-year-old church controversy by leading perhaps 10 percent of the membership away from the majority to establish a new church. Two months later, on July 4, Susan Wright died.

Suddenly faced with the collapse of church and family, the twin cornerstones of his life, Milton set about shoring up the foundations. Unable to conceive of his home without a female at its emotional core, he began the process of promoting Katharine, his 15-year-old daughter, to her mother's role, and enlisting his two youngest sons as allies and assistants in his church battles. Confident that he would still have a home to which he could return, Bishop Wright launched the first of his lawsuits against old church rivals, and set about establishing a new church.

It is important to realize that Milton had no desire to limit the intellectual growth of his children. On the contrary, he was a warm and loving father who encouraged his youngsters to stretch their minds and spirits to the fullest extent. He simply saw no reason why they could not do that while remaining at home.

In 1893, he sent Katharine off for a year at the Oberlin College Preparatory School, followed by four years at Oberlin College, where she graduated in 1898. She then returned home to Dayton to begin work as a high school teacher, and to resume her duties as female head of the Wright household.

The airplane was Wilbur and Orville's invention, but Katharine would pay a considerable price for her brothers' success. They would enjoy the benefits of life in a warm and stable family, while escaping the responsibilities that consumed the time and energy of married men. Living under their father's roof, free of the daily cares and the struggle for survival, confident in the love, support, and unquestioning loyalty of their sister, they could focus their energies on their experiments. Without those advantages, it is by no means probable that they could have succeeded. It was Katharine's most important and least recognized contribution to the invention of the airplane.

Milton had worked hard to keep his daughter at home. He was delighted when his sons made that decision on their own. Orville did not return for his senior year of high school following his mother's death in 1889. He had abandoned the regular program the year before, enrolling in special advanced courses intended to prepare recent graduates for college. As a result, he lacked several credits and would not be able to graduate with his class. It was no matter. Orville wanted to be a printer. Having apprenticed himself in a Dayton print shop for two summers, he quit school and set himself up as a job printer.

Times were hard, however. By the early 1890s a full-blown depression was under way, leading to a sudden rise in the number of young men and women who continued to live at home, waiting to inherit the family farm or business. In Orville's case, it was simply cheaper to remain in his father's house while he was working to establish himself.

Wilbur, who had spent the past three years closeted away nursing his mother, emerged from his depression during this period, but was still feeling unsure of himself. Old friends had gone off to school, set themselves up in business, and established families of their own while he had simply been marking time. He feared that college would now be a waste of money, and he did not believe that he had the temperament for success in business.

He observed the problems faced by his two older brothers with interest and sympathy. Reuchlin and Lorin were both married, and having a very difficult time making ends meet. Wilbur could not see a reason why he should do any better under the same circumstances. For the time being, he was content to work out his destiny within the safety of the family circle.

That destiny would involve a partnership with his brother Orville. Their names appeared together as the "Wright brothers" for the first time on the cover of a slim pamphlet entitled "Scenes in the Church Commission During the Last Days of Its Session," which appeared in the spring of 1888. Wilbur was the author of this strident and very professional bit of propaganda in support of his father's position in the church controversy. Orville did the printing.

The arrangement proved so successful that the printing operation quickly became a joint venture. Over the next several years they set themselves up as job printers, producing items ranging from business cards to advertising flyers. They also issued two short-lived neighborhood newspapers of very professional quality. When both of their own newspapers collapsed, the brothers underwrote the publication of a third paper edited by Orville's high school chum, the African-American poet Paul Laurence Dunbar. Aimed at Dayton's black community, it failed after three issues.

The brothers branched out in 1892, hiring help for the print shop and establishing a small bicycle repair and sales business. They continued to enjoy some success with their two businesses, and began manufacturing bicycles on a small scale in 1896. The Wright brothers were not getting rich, but they were prosperous, and able to begin building a modest bank account.

More important, the Wright brothers were now involved in two enterprises that enabled them to develop specialized skills and stretch in some very useful ways. They began to develop reputations as mechanical innovators and problem solvers of the first order. Take the case of a large printing press that Orville designed and built with Wilbur's assistance in 1889-90. Ed Sines, an old friend who helped out around the shop, recalled the reaction of a professional printer who inspected the device:

> E. C. James, I think he was pressman for a Chicago [printing] house at that time, came to the [Wright] print shop almost every time he was in the city. One day he walked into the front office and asked if "that Wright press is running today." When we told him it was running at that time, he said he would like to see it. Well, he went back into the press room, stood by the machine, looked at it, then sat down beside it, and finally crawled underneath it. After he had been under the machine for some little time, he got up and said, "Well, it works, but I certainly don't see how it does the work."

Obviously, the sort of innovative thinking involved in the design of such a printing press would play a major role in the invention of the airplane. The brothers' involvement in the bicycle trade provided further opportunities for mechanical experimentation. A self-oiling wheel hub developed by Orville offers a case in point. The brothers also designed and built a single-cylinder reciprocating engine to power the machine tools in the bicycle shop. As bicycle makers, they gained considerable experience in working with steel tubing, wood, chain, and other materials. By 1900, they had become experienced, if not professional, machinists.

Bicycling also provided them with important clues that would one day help them to unravel the intricacies of aeronautical control. Most land conveyances, from wagons to automobiles, can be controlled in only one axis of motion. In order to go around a corner, you simply turn the front wheels to the right or left. With a bicycle, however, things are much more complex. In addition to directional, or yaw, control, a rider must maintain constant balance in the roll axis to prevent himself from tipping over. The business of turning a corner requires a fairly complex coordination of control actions in both axes.

For cyclists, the business of control quickly becomes instinctive. Wilbur, however, with his gift for mechanical analysis and his ability to visualize the operation of complex systems, extracted some important lessons that would form the basis of his thinking on the all-important issue of aeronautical control.

But the years 1889-1900 provided the Wright brothers with more than just an opportunity to work with materials, learn machining skills, and stretch themselves as innovators. It gave them a chance to forge a genuine partnership, a personal bond that would enable them to work together with enormous success. In the case of the Wright brothers, the whole was greater than the sum of the parts.

Close to one another since childhood, business partners for a decade, they knew one another intimately, and developed their own very effective methods of working together to solve technical problems. It was not always easy. Outsiders sometimes mistook a discussion between the Wright brothers for a pitched battle. "Both boys had tempers," Charlie Taylor, the mechanic who assisted them in the bicycle shop, recalled many years later. "They would shout at one another something terrible. I don't think they really got mad, but they sure got awful hot!"

The arguments that shocked Charlie Taylor enabled the brothers to explore every facet of a problem. The ability of each to defend a point of view with real passion, while at the same time listening to the other fellow's opinion, was an essential part of their success. There were times when they literally argued in a circle, suddenly awakening to the fact that they had switched positions. "I love to scrap with Orv," Wilbur once remarked. "Orv is such a good scrapper."

A neighbor or friend observing Wilbur and Orville Wright in the late 1890s would have thought them a pair of fairly typical small businessmen, hardworking young fellows, honest to a fault, good

1897: *Wearing his trademark blue tick apron, Orville (at right) works in the bicycle shop alongside Ed "Jamsie" Sines, boyhood friend, classmate, and previous partner in various juvenile journalistic pursuits.*

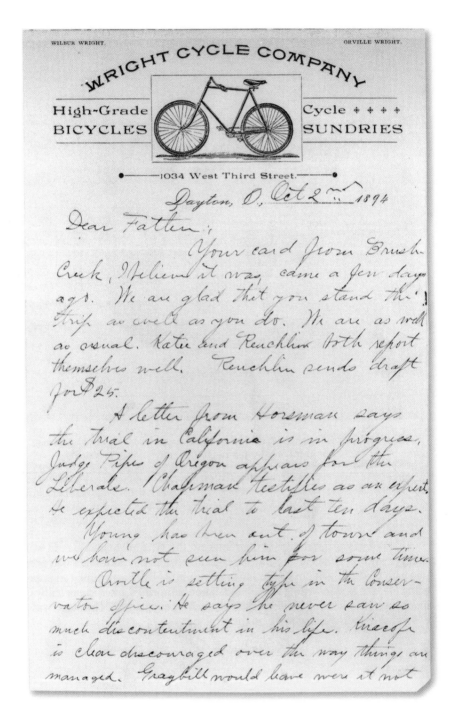

1894: *Purveyors of "high-grade bicycles" and "cycle sundries," the Wright Cycle Company stayed in business until 1907.*

During their most successful years—between 1896 and 1900—they built some 300 bicycles.

neighbors, dutiful brothers, and loving sons. Beneath that placid surface, however, the Wrights were far from satisfied with the routine of their lives.

Wilbur, in particular, continued to wrestle with the feeling that life was passing him by. He had somehow "fallen into a corner" from which he could not escape. If he was safe and secure, he had also ceased to grow. The enormous reserve of creative energy that he sensed within himself was entirely untapped. Consciously or unconsciously, he was a man in search of a challenge against which to measure himself. He found it in the airplane.

In later years, the Wrights would date their interest in flight to 1878, when their father returned from a church trip with a present for them—a small toy helicopter of the sort designed by the French aeronautical pioneer Alphonse Pénaud. They were delighted with the thing, and sent it repeatedly bumping up against the ceiling. When it broke, they built their own copies of the little toy. Thirty years later, they were still building them for the amusement of their nieces and nephews.

They never lost their boyhood interest in flight. During the 1890s, Wilbur recalled reading scattered magazine and news articles on Samuel Langley, Octave Chanute, Otto Lilienthal, and other aeronautical experimenters. They also published several stories about flying machines in the two small newspapers that they edited.

When news appeared in the Ohio newspapers of the death of the great German aeronautical pioneer Otto Lilienthal, in a glider accident in the late summer of 1896, the spark of Wilbur's interest in flight began to glow a little brighter. He spent the next three years reading what few materials he could find on the subject in the local library. Gradually, Orville began to share his interest.

One evening in the spring of 1899, Wilbur sat down at the small table where they did their writing and prepared a letter to the Smithsonian Institution, requesting additional information on flying-machine experiments. "I have been interested in the problem of mechanical and human flight ever since as a boy I constructed a number of bats of various sizes after the style of Cayley's and Pénaud's machines," he explained. "My observations since have only convinced me more firmly that human flight is possible and practicable." It was, he believed, "only a question of knowledge and skill." The success, when it came, would not be the work of any one person. Rather, "the experiments and investigations of a large number of independent workers will result in the accumulation of information and knowledge and skill which will finally lead to accomplished flight." Wilbur hastened to assure Smithsonian officials that he was a serious man. "I am an enthusiast," he admitted, "but not a crank in the sense that I have some pet theories as to the proper construction of a flying machine." He wished only to avail himself "of all that is already known and then if possible add my mite to help on the future worker who will attain final success." Over the next five years he would achieve a great deal more than that.

1897: Orville, still clean-shaven and boasting a full head of hair, was painfully shy in public but could be a practical joker among friends and family. Here he is still recovering from the attack of typhoid that nearly killed him.

1897: Wilbur had a countenance "remarkable, curious," according to a French observer, the head of "a bird, long and bony, and with a long nose....
The eye is a superb blue-gray, with tints of gold that bespeak an ardent flame."

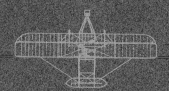

I CANNOT THINK OF ANY PART

BIRD FLIGHT HAD IN THE

DEVELOPMENT OF HUMAN FLIGHT

EXCEPTING AS AN INSPIRATION....

AFTER WE HAD THOUGHT OUT

CERTAIN PRINCIPLES, WE THEN

WATCHED THE BIRD....

IN A FEW CASES WE DID DETECT THE

SAME THING IN THE BIRD'S FLIGHT.

Orville Wright

2

BUILDING
WINGS

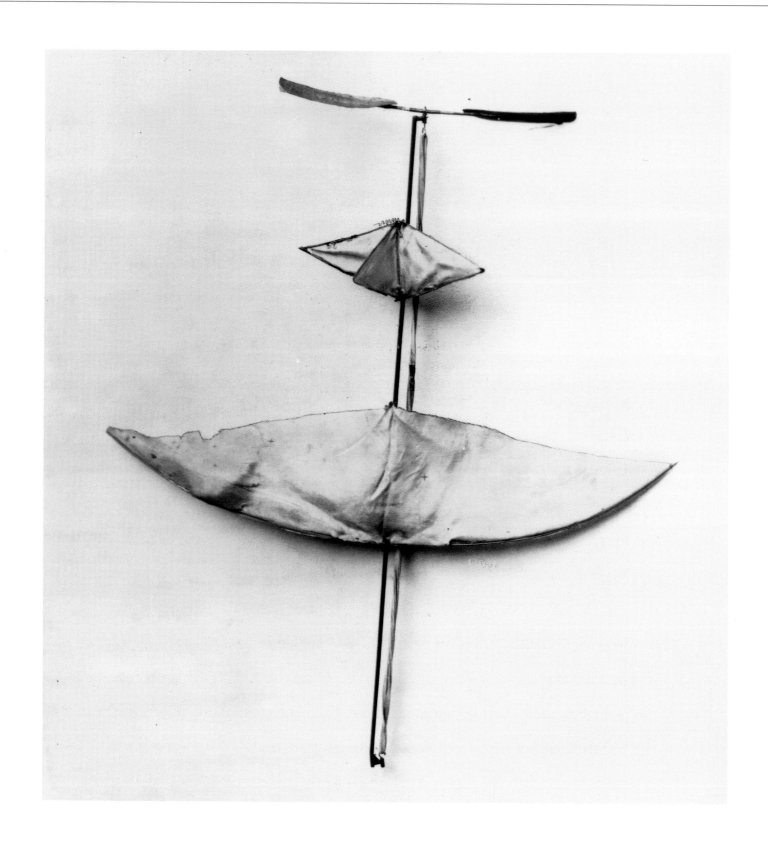

1871: *French aeronautical experimenter Alphonse Pénaud's glider, the* Planophore, *was the first model airplane powered with twisted strands of rubber.*

T HE WRIGHT BROTHERS' INITIAL design concepts for a flying machine blossomed into the famous flights at Kitty Hawk in less than five years. They accomplished this feat with little assistance and while running a successful business. What was the source of this achievement? On first glance, it would seem "sheer genius" lay at the heart of their success. The brothers certainly were gifted people, and their reputation as towering figures of invention is much deserved. Yet their genius is reflected not only in the craft that carried them into the air on that chilly windswept day in December 1903 but also in the approach they evolved and employed to create the technology of flight. In the case of Wilbur and Orville, a number of specific research techniques, innate engineering skills, and personality traits came together in a unique way and largely explain why these two men succeeded in inventing the airplane. The reasons behind the brothers' rapid and startling success can be traced with a careful look at the Wrights' inventive methodology. In some ways, understanding that methodology makes their world-changing accomplishment even more impressive. Strict engineering techniques were central to the Wright brothers' approach to mechanical flight. They rejected the uninformed trial-and-error methods so many of their contemporaries practiced. Like all good engineers, their first step was to familiarize themselves with the work of previous experimenters. Wilbur and Orville did have some knowledge of the field before they began serious aeronautical research of their own. In addition to a bit of general reading about flight, they had played with kites and other flying toys as kids. And, in the last years of the 19th century, as newspapers and popular periodicals covered the exploits of the growing community of aeronautical pioneers, the Wrights avidly kept up with their progress. By 1899, the brothers' casual observance of the work of others had transformed into an earnest study of flight.

The first formal expression of the brothers' desire to embark on serious flight research was the eloquent letter requesting information on the topic that Wilbur wrote to the Smithsonian Institution on May 30, 1899. Of the reference works suggested by the Smithsonian, two were particularly valuable. Octave Chanute's *Progress in Flying Machines,* published in 1894, and the *Aeronautical Annual* for 1895, 1896, and 1897, edited by James Means, provided a compendium of virtually everything that had been done with heavier-than-air flying machines up to Otto Lilienthal's fatal accident in 1896. The scattered and isolated efforts of those attempting to get into the air were compiled in an accessible, comprehensive set of publications. The newcomer to aeronautics hardly had to look elsewhere to get started. Wilbur and Orville devoured these helpful books, along with other material the Smithsonian sent them and what they acquired from additional sources.

Historians typically suggest that the Wrights' literature search yielded little truly useful information to build on and that the brothers were surprised at how little had been accomplished in light of how many capable people had worked on the problem of flight and how long it had been a subject of inquiry. It was true that most of the critical questions still remained unanswered by this time, but the Wrights benefited from their survey of the still nascent field of aeronautics in a number of areas. Certain concepts about wing shapes and stability, the basic aerodynamic formulae for calculating lift and drag, and fundamental engineering data with regard to materials and sizing needed to design the structure of their flying machines were all in place when the Wrights took up the problem of flight. When the brothers entered the scene, they rapidly made conceptual breakthroughs that raised aeronautics to a completely new level. But these strides were possible in part because of the foundation built by previous experimentation.

Despite the age-old human desire to fly, it was only during the 19th century that real advancement was made. The critical turning point came with the work of an English baronet named Sir George Cayley. Working throughout the first half of the 19th century, Cayley had mounted a well-conceived, systematic program of aeronautical research and experimentation. His most significant conceptual

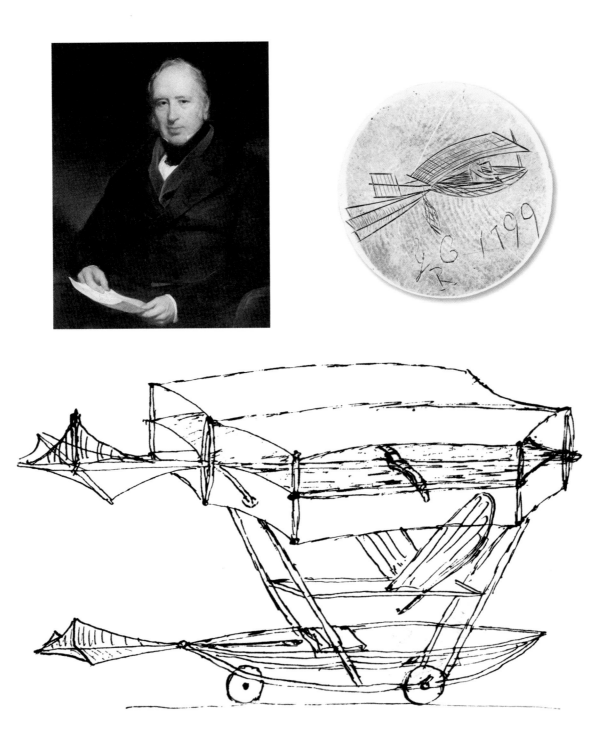

Sir George Cayley (upper left) described a modern airplane as a machine with fixed wings, a fuselage, and a tail, with separate systems to provide lift, propulsion, and control. His drawing of his Boy Carrier *illustrates his idea (lower); in 1799 he commemorated his concept with a silver disk (upper right).*

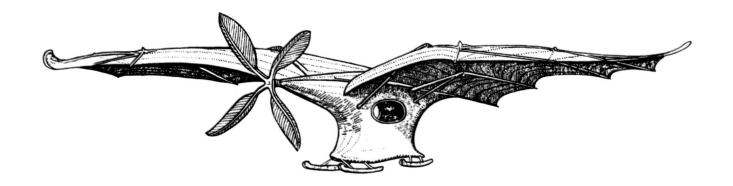

1890: *Distinguished French electrical engineer Clément Ader attempted to fly the steam-powered, bat-winged* Éole *(upper).*

1894: *Sir Hiram Maxim's four-ton steam-powered biplane rose a few inches from its track before crashing.*

breakthrough, which was key to the creation of the modern airplane, was his definition of the airplane as a machine with fixed wings, a fuselage, and a tail, with separate systems to provide lift, propulsion, and control. Cayley built and flew the world's first successful model glider in 1804. Later, he designed and constructed two full-size gliders capable of brief flights with a pilot on board. He also published the results of his research in major scientific journals of the day. Breaking with the fanciful and romantic conceptions that had dominated aeronautical thinking for centuries, he established the serious, experimentally based study of mechanical flight that would eventually lead to the success of Wilbur and Orville Wright in December 1903. For his efforts, Cayley was often referred to as the "Father of Aerial Navigation."

As important as the steps Cayley took were, many daunting conceptual and technical challenges still had to be overcome to realize a practical flying machine. Attempts at imitating the flight of birds had led nowhere, but in the immediate pre-Wright period, aeronautical research matured and became better organized. Three distinct approaches emerged among experimenters: Those who built powered, full-size, piloted aircraft from the outset; researchers who thought the best approach was to begin with small models; and others who chose to experiment with full-size gliders as a preliminary step to powered flight.

For the first group, propulsion was the central focus. They believed that the development of a powerful, lightweight aeronautical engine was the last significant obstacle to human flight. Clément Ader, a distinguished French electrical engineer who was a pioneer in the development of the telephone, was among the best known experimenters in this camp. He attempted to fly a batlike craft called the *Éole* in October 1890. The aerodynamics of his airplane were poorly thought out, and he had a completely unworkable means of controlling it, should the aircraft somehow get off the ground. The *Éole's* powerful, lightweight steam engine was its only noteworthy feature. Ader made an uncontrolled hop of 165 feet at an altitude of eight inches with the airplane. He had indeed demonstrated that, with enough power, a winged craft could be coaxed aloft for a short leap into the air. But the *Éole* was devoid of all the other elements necessary for a practical flying machine and contributed little to the eventual achievement of human mechanical flight.

Sir Hiram Maxim, an expatriate American living in England who earlier achieved fame as the inventor of the machine gun, pursued a path similar to Ader. "Without doubt the motor is the chief thing to be considered," Maxim asserted in 1892. "Scientists have long said, Give us a motor and we will very soon give you a successful flying machine."

Maxim built a huge, four-ton biplane fitted with two very efficient 180-horsepower steam engines, each turning an 18-foot propeller. The aircraft rode on an elaborate track with guard rails to prevent it from rising more than a few inches. It was hardly more than a complicated engine test rig. On its final trial, on July 31, 1894, it traveled 600 feet down the track, reaching a speed of 42 miles per hour. It rose slightly, broke from the guardrails, and crashed. Like Ader and his *Éole,* all Maxim accomplished was to show that a powerful engine could briefly lift a crude aircraft into the air. There was little more that could be learned from the experiment.

MODEL AIRCRAFT SEEMED AN OBVIOUS ALTERNATIVE TO THE COMPLEX, EXPENSIVE avenue of flight research conducted by people such as Ader and Maxim. Although Cayley first demonstrated the value of these small, inexpensive research tools with his classic model glider of 1804, a French marine engineer named Alphonse Pénaud was by far the most influential of the model experimenters. In 1871, Pénaud built and publicly flew a small, rubber-powered monoplane glider he called the *Planophore.* The *Planophore* demonstrated the important concept of aircraft stability and was a crucial link between the work of Cayley and the modern airplane.

Another of Pénaud's contributions was the use of twisted strands of rubber to power his models, a technique that no doubt helped spur childhood interest in aviation in every generation since. Pénaud inspired many who later contributed greatly to the invention of the airplane, including the Wright brothers. Wilbur and Orville credited him as one of their most important predecessors. Pénaud was confined to a wheelchair at a young age because of a debilitating hip disease. Frustrated and in ill health, sadly he took his own life at the youthful age of 30, in 1880.

Building and flying full-size, piloted gliders proved to be the most viable path of flight research in the late 19th century, and it was the avenue the Wright brothers chose. George Cayley again established a precedent. In 1849, a glider he designed called the *Boy Carrier* made a brief flight of a few yards. Little more than a leap into the air, it was still the first time in history that a human being was carried aloft in a heavier-than-air craft. The *Coachman Carrier,* a second Cayley glider, made another short flight in 1853.

A professionally trained German engineer named Otto Lilienthal was the most important and influential pioneer of all those who were experimenting with glider flight in the 19th century. After serving in the military in the Franco-Prussian War, Lilienthal established himself as a successful engineer.

By 1880 he had begun manufacturing small steam engines and marine foghorns, among other things.

Lilienthal first began aeronautical experimentation as far back as the 1860s. After two decades of imaginative research, he produced the most complete and accurate body of aerodynamic data up to that time. He also showed beyond doubt that a curved wing profile produced optimum lift. Lilienthal published his important aerodynamic research in *Der Vogelflug als Grundlage der Fliegekunst (Bird Flight as the Basis of Aviation)* in 1889, and in several other articles. The size wing required to support a given weight at a particular velocity could easily be calculated from Lilienthal's results. From then on, all serious turn-of-the-century aeronautical experimenters used his work as a starting point.

Lilienthal's next step was to build full-size, piloted gliders based on his impressive program of aerodynamic research. He produced a series of 16 different elegant designs from 1891 to 1896 and made close to 2,000 brief flights in them. The gliders' wings, ranging in area from ten to twenty square meters, could be folded to the rear for easier transport and storage. Lilienthal controlled his craft by shifting his body weight to alter the center of gravity. Cradling himself vertically in a harness suspended below an elliptical opening in the wings, he would swing his legs from side to side and fore and aft to maintain equilibrium. Lilienthal could stay in the air for 12 to 15 seconds and travel more than a thousand feet in his gliders. A Boston news correspondent made an enthusiastic assessment of Lilienthal's aircraft: "Here was a flying machine, not constructed by a crank … but by an engineer of ability.… A machine not made to look at, but to fly with."

Lilienthal's aeronautical experiments came to a sudden end on August 9, 1896, while he was soaring in one of his monoplane gliders. A strong gust of wind caused the craft to nose up sharply, stall, and crash from an altitude of 50 feet. Lilienthal broke his spine and died from his injuries the next day in a Berlin hospital.

Although his aircraft were only a stepping-stone toward the realization of successful powered flight, Lilienthal's progress was substantial. His contributions to aerodynamics and practical aircraft design were the most important since Cayley's experiments in the first half of the 19th century. Lilienthal was the first to gain extensive flying experience with aircraft designed on a foundation of carefully collected, sound aeronautical data. He was the Wright brothers' primary role model when they began their serious aeronautical experimentation in 1899. They followed his precise engineering approach and adopted his method of gaining actual flying experience in full-size gliders. Wilbur would later refer to Lilienthal as "the greatest of the precursors."

Exciting and promising strides were made toward the invention of a successful powered airplane in the late 1890s. But as the century drew to a close, the freedom of movement teasingly displayed by nature's winged creatures was still far from a reality for humans. What was needed at this point was someone to assimilate the significant research and experience amassed by Lilienthal and others and make the necessary set of conceptual leaps that would transform aeronautics from fitful, though at times impressive, bounds into the air into a genuine understanding and resolution of the complex set of problems mechanical flight presented.

The experimenters who met this challenge were, of course, Wilbur and Orville Wright. They raised the field of aeronautics to an entirely new level with their highly developed engineering acumen and uncommon problem-solving insight. As original and pathbreaking as the Wrights' achievement was, they did not work in isolation; equally important, they entered the field at a propitious moment. Had the brothers been a generation older, it is not at all certain that they would have avoided the stumbling blocks of their predecessors. Although the Wright brothers unquestionably possessed extraordinary talents, their genius lay as much in their insightful analysis and adaptation of what had come before them as it did in their own innate creativity.

In the course of reviewing the century of experimentation conducted since Cayley's breakthrough ideas and research, the Wrights identified the remaining obstacles to human flight. Building on Cayley, they considered three essential areas. First, a successful flying machine would certainly require a set of sustaining surfaces of some kind, wings being the obvious form. Second, an airplane needed a way of propelling itself through the air. The third requirement would be a method of balancing and controlling the aircraft in flight.

Most experimenters working before the Wrights ran into trouble because they failed to think in terms of the entire set of problems from the start. They focused on isolated aspects of aircraft design without a clear idea of how their work ultimately would be integrated into a practical, powered airplane. The Wrights were the first to recognize that all three of the core requirements pointed out by Cayley had to be addressed with an eye to building a powered flying machine in its final form. Stopgap aircraft that incorporated a solution to only one of the key elements had no chance of success.

Of the three broad categories of flight research, the Wrights initially gave the most consideration to control. Propulsion seemed relatively less problematic. By this time, lightweight steam engines were fairly prevalent, as were pioneering efforts with gasoline engines. If and when they were ever ready to begin making powered flights, Wilbur and Orville thought it likely they would be able to purchase a suitable power source, or make one on their own.

Some valuable work also had been completed on wing shapes and profiles and aircraft structures by the time the brothers started their own research. Otto Lilienthal's lift data and work with curved wing surfaces provided a sound starting point for Wilbur and Orville. The structural design of Octave

1895: German aeronautical engineer Otto Lilienthal flies a biplane glider of his own design. Between 1891 and 1896 he made nearly 2,000 flights in 16 different kinds of gliders—most simple monoplanes.

*1895: Bystanders watch as Lilienthal makes another successful
glide. Wilbur called him the "greatest of the precursors."*

Chanute and Augustus Herring's classic biplane glider of 1896 provided a useful pattern for the Wrights' beginning structural layout.

Unlike aerodynamics and structures, preliminary work on balance and control barely had been addressed by previous experimenters. Seeing this as the most glaring shortcoming of the work performed so far, the Wrights first concentrated on the problem of control. Wilbur summed up the brothers' view in a 1901 speech: "When this one feature has been worked out the age of flying machines will have arrived, for all other difficulties are of minor importance."

Of those who had considered control at all, most had only the vaguest sense of the relationship between maintaining stability in the air and steering the craft. Generally, they gave no thought whatsoever to controlling their machines once airborne. Typically, they focused on incorporating some form of inherent stability that, independent of the pilot, would return the aircraft to equilibrium if a gust of wind or some other force upset it. Just getting airborne was enough to begin with, they reasoned, and if simple, stable, straight-line flight was accomplished, steering could be easily dealt with later.

Somewhat surprisingly, few recognized that this was dead-end thinking. As we know today, it is possible to fly either a stable or an unstable aircraft. But no aircraft can fly without an adequate means of control. The Wright brothers' aircraft were, in fact, unstable vehicles, but they were fully controllable by the pilot and as a result capable of practical flight.

The control system had to be an integral part of the design from the outset for any chance of success. The Wrights alone recognized this and were quite frankly puzzled by the failure of so many of their peers to grasp this concept. The brothers' recognition of the centrality of control to mechanical flight was among the most significant, if not the premier, conceptual leap that set them apart from all their predecessors.

The Wrights also were the first to see that control was not merely an adjunct to stability, but the essence of maintaining equilibrium. Their extensive experience with bicycles contributed to their understanding of this relationship. Despite being a completely unstable machine, a bicycle can be easily controlled by the rider. The bicycle provided a familiar illustration to the Wrights that instability and control are not mutually exclusive. Thus, they did not share the concern of many of their aeronautical peers about sacrificing stability in an aircraft. A cyclist must make constant control movements to keep upright; so too must an airplane pilot exercise similar authority over his craft to stay in the air. Further, the bicycle demonstrated that superhuman reflexes or extraordinary movements were not required to control instability. It was not unreasonable to think the same could be true of an airplane.

Wilbur and Orville gravitated toward the work of Lilienthal not only because his aerodynamic data provided a sound foundation from which to begin, but also because they were in complete agreement with his approach of gaining actual flying experience in full-size gliders. Though rarely noted, one of the most significant aspects of the Wrights' inventive work, apart from designing and building the airplane itself, was that the brothers had to teach themselves how to fly in the process. Working from the premise that their airplane would have to be controlled, that it would not be an inherently stable craft, they knew that they would have to develop the skills to operate such a complex machine. Wilbur drew a parallel to an uninitiated rider mounting an untamed horse:

> Now, there are two ways of learning how to ride a fractious horse: one is to get on him and learn by actual practice how each motion and trick may be best met; the other is to sit on a fence and watch the beast a while, and then retire to the house and at leisure figure out the best way of overcoming his jumps and kicks. The latter system is the safest; but the former, on the whole, turns out the larger proportion of good riders. It is very much the same in learning to ride a flying machine; if you are looking for perfect safety, you will do well to sit on a fence and watch the birds; but if you really wish to learn, you must mount a machine and become acquainted with its tricks by actual trial.

They understood that learning to be pilots would be just as important as building a technically successful airplane.

T HE WRIGHT BROTHERS COMPLETED THEIR FIRST EXPERIMENTAL AIRCRAFT IN JUST A FEW weeks after receiving the material and references supplied by the Smithsonian Institution. It was not a full-size glider. Rather, they started by constructing a small kite to evaluate the method of control they planned to use in their first man-carrying craft.

The first obvious requirement was a means of keeping the wings level. The Wrights decided to maintain lateral balance by independently altering the angle at which each wing half attacked the air. If one wing half is presented at a greater angle to the wind than the other, it will generate more lift, cause that side of the airplane to rise, and result in a banking of the entire machine. With this technique, the pilot could not only maintain equilibrium but also initiate controlled turns.

The Wrights achieved the differential in the angle to the wind of each wing half by twisting, or

1896: *Augustus Herring takes the pilot's position in the influential Chanute-Herring "two-surface" machine. Chanute (top) became an enthusiastic friend and supporter of the Wrights, even joining them at Kitty Hawk.*

warping, the wing tips of their craft in opposite directions. The pilot would operate the wing warping via lines attached to the outer edges of the wing structure. This simple and elegant means of generating greater lift on one side of the supporting surfaces to maintain equilibrium and induce turns was a key aspect of the Wrights' invention. Virtually all successful airplanes use the concept of differential lift to turn, be it with wing-warping or with movable surfaces, called ailerons, attached to the rear edge of the wings. It was the central feature of the Wright brothers' patent on the airplane.

Even though wing-warping was such a key element of the Wright airplane, the precise origin of the idea remains somewhat unclear. It is one of those aspects of the brothers' work that has to a degree fallen between the cracks of their contemporary correspondence and recordkeeping, and the Wrights' own recounting of the sequence of events in later years does not explain it.

In a letter written to Octave Chanute on May 13, 1900, Wilbur indicated that the observation of birds was the source for the principle of angling the wings in opposite directions for lateral control:

> My observation of the flight of buzzards leads me to believe that they regain their lateral balance, when partly overturned by a gust of wind, by a torsion of the tips of the wings. If the rear edge of the right wing tip is twisted upward and the left downward the bird becomes an animated windmill and instantly begins a turn, a line from its head to its tail being the axis.

When asked years later, long after Wilbur's death, about the influence bird flight had on their work, Orville claimed it contributed little.

> I cannot think of any part bird flight had in the development of human flight excepting as an inspiration. Although we intently watched birds fly in a hope of learning something from them I cannot think of anything that was first learned in that way. After we had thought out certain principles, we then watched the bird to see whether it used the same principles. In a few cases we did detect the same thing in the bird's flight.
>
> Learning the secret of flight from a bird was a good deal like learning the secret of magic from a magician. After you once know the trick and know what to look for you see things that you did not notice when you did not know exactly what to look for.

However the Wrights came upon the idea, whether it was through the observation of birds or conceiving it on their own without any external model, their taking advantage of the "dynamic reactions of the air instead of shifting weight" for control, as Wilbur put it, was a conceptual leap of immeasurable consequence.

To make wing-warping practical the brothers now had to develop a structural design with which they could easily twist the wings yet not compromise the physical integrity of the airframe. They initially thought of pivoting the wings through an arrangement of shafts and gears, but that was too heavy and impractical. A better possibility came to mind while Wilbur was minding the bicycle shop one day. After making a sale of an inner tube for a tire, he removed the inner tube from the cardboard box in which it was packaged. While absentmindedly twisting the box between his fingers as he chatted with his customer, Wilbur noticed that even when he applied considerable torsion across the box it retained its lateral stiffness. It occurred to him that the same result could be achieved with a set of properly rigged airplane wings. (Interestingly, when the Wrights were later seeking their patent, they used the same cardboard box analogy to illustrate the wing-warping principle to a confused Patent Office examiner reviewing their application. Wilbur in fact sent the examiner a bicycle inner tube box to try the twisting action for himself.)

WHILE READING ABOUT THE WORK OF EARLIER EXPERIMENTERS, THE WRIGHTS HAD become familiar with a number of multiwing designs for lifting surfaces. The bicycle inner tube box logically suggested a biplane configuration as an obvious form to which the torsion principle could be applied. Among the most significant aircraft of the pre-Wright era was a biplane hang glider developed in 1896 by Octave Chanute and Augustus Herring. It was known as the "two-surface" and it had made flights nearly as long as Lilienthal had achieved with his glider.

The way in which the Chanute-Herring biplane was braced was of particular interest. Chanute was an accomplished civil engineer and bridge builder and was therefore very familiar with the Pratt truss, then commonly used in bridge construction. It consisted of a crisscross arrangement of steel wires between the open bays of the bridge's frame that resulted in a simple, but extremely rigid, structure. Chanute utilized the same crossed wire system to support the framework of his biplane glider.

The trussed biplane was an ideal structural form for the Wrights' wing-warping concept. It had the necessary structural rigidity and at the same time could be easily flexed for lateral control. To accomplish the lateral flexibility, however, the Wrights had to make one crucial modification to the Chanute-Herring-type biplane. The span-wise trussing would be retained, but the fore-and-aft diagonal wire bracing had to be removed. Rigged in this way, the airframe would take on precisely the same characteristics as the cardboard box with its ends removed. The wings could be twisted across the chord (chord refers to the width of the wing) without loss of strength and stiffness along the length of the wing. The design was simple and elegant, as it required no complex or heavy mechanism to achieve lateral control.

To test their wing-warping concept and structural design, the Wrights built a small, five-foot-span biplane kite in the summer of 1899. The vertical uprights that supported the wing panels one above the other were trussed rigidly across the front and rear of the biplane wing cell in the manner of the Chanute-Herring glider. Across the chord—looking end on, in other words—the kite was left unbraced to allow for warping. To manipulate the wing warping, four lines were attached to the top and bottom of the front, outer uprights, with the other ends of the lines connected to a pair of sticks held by the operator. When the sticks were tilted in opposite directions, the tension on the lines imparted the twist on the wings, providing lateral control. The kite could also be controlled in climb and descent by a flat horizontal surface attached to the center upright. When both sticks were tilted in the same direction, the surface changed its angle to the wind, resulting in a change in attitude of the kite.

It is not known precisely when the kite was tested, but Wilbur flew it sometime in late July or early August 1899. A group of schoolboys flying their own kites witnessed the tests at a nearby field and were fascinated by the strange-looking craft, as well as the adult in business attire who had joined them to "play." The kite responded quickly and precisely to Wilbur's commands, confirming the soundness of the brothers' lateral-control concept. It was readily apparent that wing-warping was far superior to any of the crude methods of control previously used by others, including Lilienthal's weight shifting. The Wrights' seminal 1899 kite, with its biplane configuration, modified Pratt truss bracing, and rudimentary wing-warping control system for lateral balance, formed the nucleus of the flying machine that would successfully carry a human being into the air over the isolated beach at Kitty Hawk in 1903.

With the results of the 1899 kite so encouraging, Wilbur and Orville felt they were ready to move to a full-size, piloted glider incorporating their wing-warping system of lateral control. Despite the quick start, an entire year of planning and designing would pass before the brothers actually began to construct their first man-carrying aircraft. Having made several promising steps toward mechanical flight with their relatively simple model kite, the Wrights were now confronted with a wide array of complicated technical problems and seemingly mysterious physical forces. Before the goal of human flight could be realized, the Wrights would have to master innumerable challenges with regard to aerodynamics, structures, control, and propulsion, not to mention having to avoid breaking their necks in

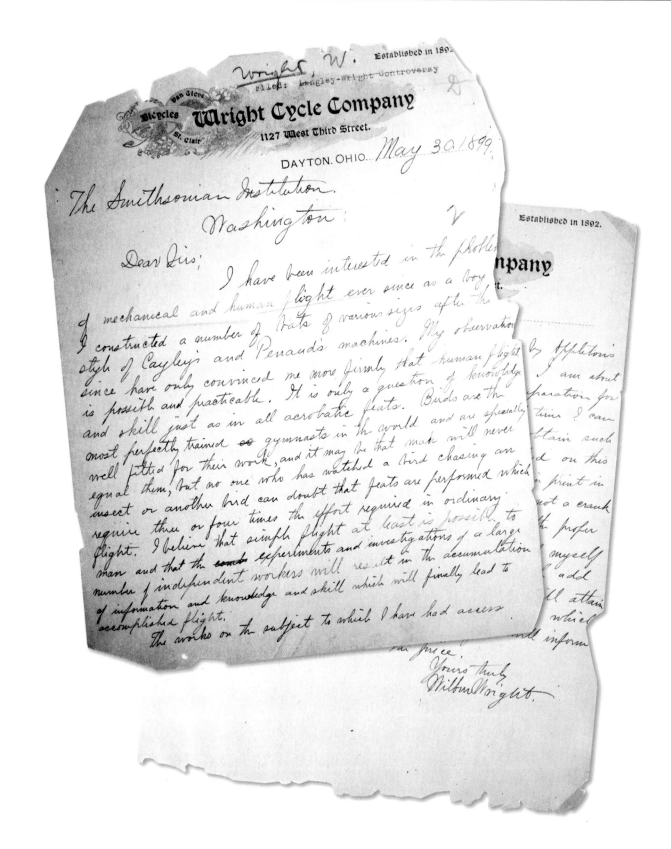

I HAVE BEEN INTERESTED IN THE PROBLEM OF

MECHANICAL AND HUMAN FLIGHT EVER SINCE AS A

BOY I CONSTRUCTED A NUMBER OF BATS....

MY OBSERVATIONS SINCE HAVE ONLY CONVINCED

ME MORE FIRMLY THAT HUMAN FLIGHT IS POSSIBLE

AND PRACTICABLE .... I AM AN ENTHUSIAST, BUT

NOT A CRANK IN THE SENSE THAT I HAVE SOME PET

THEORIES AS TO THE PROPER CONSTRUCTION

OF A FLYING MACHINE. I WISH TO AVAIL MYSELF OF

ALL THAT IS ALREADY KNOWN AND THEN IF

POSSIBLE ADD MY MITE TO HELP ON THE FUTURE

WORKER WHO WILL ATTAIN FINAL SUCCESS.

Wilbur Wright 1899

Letter to Smithsonian Institution (opposite) requesting information the process. Wilbur and Orville now engaged in the monumental challenge of transforming these beginning concepts into a fully developed, practical piece of technology.

The Wright brothers possessed a number of highly developed conceptual skills and innate engineering talents that enabled them to accomplish these tasks successfully and move ahead of the rest of the aeronautical community quickly. Their initial definition of the essential barriers to mechanical flight and the design of their 1899 kite reveal many of them. Their extraordinary ability to turn abstract conceptual models of a complex problem into practical, concrete technology was perhaps the single most important skill they brought to their inventive work. This was at the heart of their development of the wing-warping control system. The Wrights moved deftly from the imaginative theoretical idea of differential lift on opposite sides of the wing to achieve lateral balance to the simple and workable scheme of twisting the wing panels in alternate directions. They skillfully merged an abstract intellectual concept for control with a practical understanding of structures and materials to produce an imaginative, effective solution to a fundamental problem. This problem solving process was key to their overall inventive success.

VISUAL THINKING AND A CAPACITY FOR MANIPULATION OF MENTAL IMAGERY ARE CRITICAL tools for conceptualizing engineering solutions in this way. Even though there may be fundamental mathematical relationships or articulated scientific principles that underlie the creation of a new machine or structure, invariably a distinct facet of the design is aesthetic in nature, an aspect that results from the maker's particular sense of what will or will not work, or what "looks" right or wrong. This aesthetic element is not limited merely to the object's appearance. The more important element involves the technical feasibility and physical arrangement of components that leads to the success or failure of the design. Especially creative and productive inventors and engineers can visualize an object in their mind, and with great facility, turn it over, form new images of it, incorporate old forms from other designs, and finally come up either with a much improved device or with something totally original that will accomplish new goals. The designer literally has a vision of what the object or structure should look like and how it will work. The great extent to which the Wrights themselves used mental imagery and nonverbal thought to conceptualize basic structures and mechanisms, even aerodynamic theories, figured prominently in their steps toward powered flight. It was among the most prevalent and important aspects of their inventive method.

Continuity of design was another hallmark of the Wright brothers' approach to aeronautical engineering. Each of their gliders and each powered aircraft stemmed from a single evolving design that incorporated what was learned from the previous craft. They followed a coherent program of experimental development rather than simply building a series of individual aircraft. So many of their predecessors went from one completely different design to the next, a methodology that was rarely productive.

The Wrights understood that an airplane was a complex system of interdependent technological elements. They recognized that they must not allow their attention to be focused too much on any one of these elements to the neglect of the others. The design of a working airplane demanded persistent attention to the overall goal, and, unlike other aeronautical experimenters, they believed that no specific component was more important than any other. No matter how advanced the wing, without an adequate control system, the aircraft would not fly. No matter how effective the control system, without a sound structural design to carry the flight loads, the aircraft would not fly. Wilbur and Orville understood that an airplane is not a single device but a series of distinct mechanical and structural entities that, when working in proper unison, create a machine capable of flight. They also realized that the pilot is a part of this system and therefore gave as much attention to learning to fly their aircraft as they did to designing and building them.

Technology transfer was another factor. The Wrights made good use of their knowledge of other seemingly unrelated technologies. Concepts—at times even basic hardware itself—were drawn from other technical areas and incorporated into their aeronautical work. The role of bicycles is a clear case. It is typically noted that the Wright brothers were bicycle mechanics, but rarely explained is how their familiarity with that technology influenced their aeronautical work. In the late 19th century, some followers of aeronautical progress in fact had suggested bicycle makers might very well be linked to the eventual development of a practical airplane. One such forecaster, James Means, editor of the widely read aviation journal the *Aeronautical Annual,* published an article in the 1896 edition pointing to the links between bicycles and airplanes. "'Wheeling is just like flying!'" he wrote. "To learn to wheel one must learn to balance; to learn to fly one must learn to balance."

At every critical juncture in the Wrights' journey to practical flight, these innate skills and approaches to invention are readily apparent. Wilbur and Orville were far more than fine mechanics who managed to coax a flying machine into the air. They engineered a fundamentally original technology using techniques and talents common to the most creative inventors of their era.

The 1899 kite took the brothers a long way in addressing the question of control. The following year they began to design and build their first full-size, piloted glider. Next they turned their attention to aerodynamics. It was one thing to create a set of lifting surfaces for a small kite. It was quite another to build a large, heavy glider, climb aboard, and launch oneself into the air. They now had to consider seriously such design elements as the shape of the wing outline and the precise curvature of the wing profile. They also had to determine the wing area required to lift the weight of the craft and the pilot and the type and size of construction materials.

For the basic structural layout of the glider, they again used the trussed biplane-wing arrangement developed for the earlier wing-warping kite. Designing the proper shape for the wing profile, known as the airfoil, was critical. Lilienthal had proved the superior efficiency of curved airfoils over flat wings, but how deep should the curve be?

The second critical aerodynamic issue dealt with the phenomenon known as the movement of the center of pressure. The center of pressure is the focal point of the lifting force acting on a wing in flight. As the angle of the wing to the oncoming flow of air changes, the center of pressure moves along the chord, or width, of the wing. In the case of a curved surface, such as an airplane wing, the movement of the center of pressure reverses the direction of its travel when the wing approaches a level position parallel to the direction of the airflow.

Most early experimenters built their aircraft without knowing that the center of pressure behaved in this way on a curved surface. The Wrights, on the other hand, carefully thought about the airflow over the wing before fabricating any component of their glider. They reasoned that the center of pressure had to reverse with a curved surface when it approached the horizontal because, unlike a flat plate, part of the top surface would now be exposed to the wind, generating an added downward pressure. Since the center of pressure is the point about which the overall pressure on the wing surface balances, the direction of its travel would be affected when a new component of pressure, oriented in the opposite direction, was introduced.

An airplane is at equilibrium when the position of the center of pressure and the center of gravity of the aircraft coincide. When they do not, the machine will pitch up or down, depending on whether the center of pressure is in front of or behind the center of gravity. It is difficult to keep the center of pressure close to the center of gravity, because it moves about quite freely in response to slight changes in the attitude of the wings. Wilbur summed up the dilemma this way:

> The balancing of a gliding or flying machine is very simple in theory. It merely consists in causing the center of pressure to coincide with the center of gravity. But in actual practice there seems to be an almost boundless incompatibility of temper which prevents their remaining peaceably

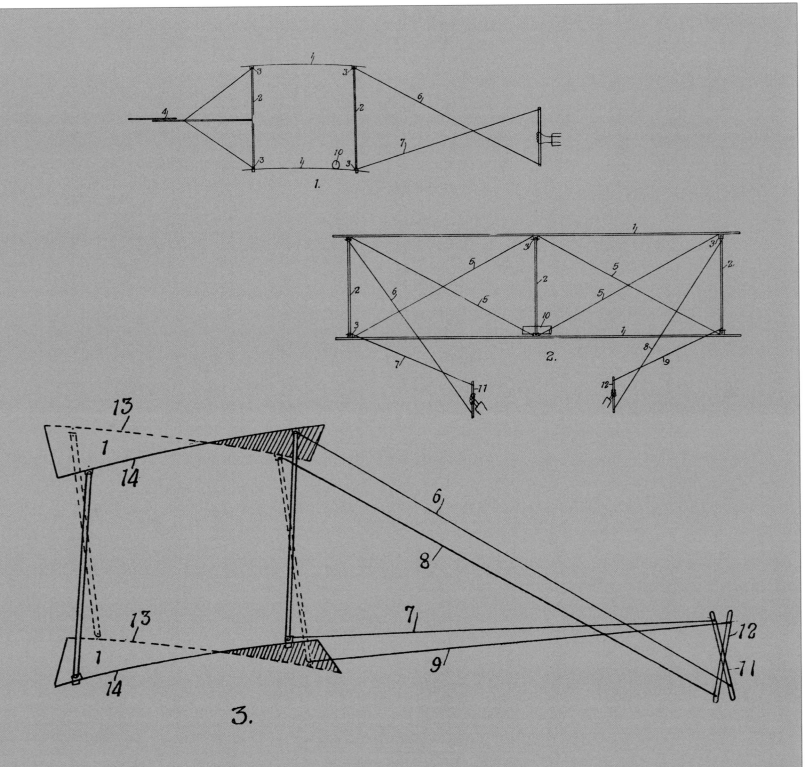

1.

2.

3.

The Wright brothers constructed their 1899 kite to explore the effectiveness of wing warping.

By removing the fore-and-aft crossbracing they found the wings could be warped.

AIRFLOW >

▲ **CENTER OF PRESSURE**
on curved surface moves with angle of attack

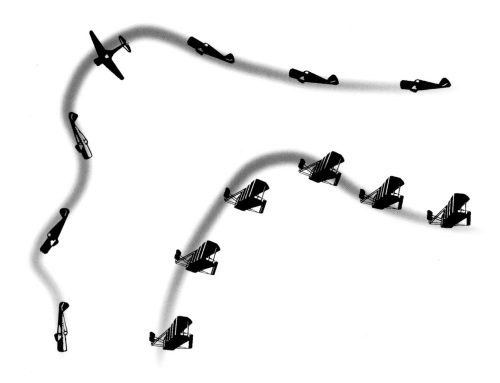

Diagram (top) shows that when a wing's angle of attack is decreased with a curved surface, the center of pressure moves forward. Bottom, the Wrights' placement of the canard in the front allowed an aircraft to parachute down in the case of a stall (right), rather than nosedive as it would with a rear-tail configuration (left).

together for a single instant, so that the operator, who in this case acts as peacemaker, often suffers injury to himself while attempting to bring them together.

Otto Lilienthal tried to keep up with the constantly changing position of the center of pressure with his weight-shifting technique. He kept his gliders level by swinging his legs back and forth, which constantly changed the center of gravity of the craft to coincide with the changing center of pressure. This approach required incredible acrobatic movements and ultimately cost Lilienthal his life.

The Wrights realized that it was highly impractical to keep the center of pressure and the center of gravity balanced by shifting body weight. It would be far easier, they thought, to control the movement of the center of pressure aerodynamically in relation to a fixed center of gravity. Since the center of pressure moves as the wing changes its angle to the oncoming flow of air, if the wings remain at a reasonably constant attitude, the center of pressure will be fairly steady. A steady center of pressure balanced with the fixed center of gravity would maintain the aircraft in level flight.

To control the attitude of the wings, the brothers mounted a horizontal surface just ahead of them. The pilot could flex the surface, now called an elevator, in either direction with a lever. If the aircraft rose because the center of pressure on the bottom of the wing moved ahead of the center of gravity of the glider, the elevator could be turned so that its top surface faced the wind. The downward pressure of the wind on the elevator would counteract the upward pressure acting on the wings and cause the glider to level itself. Conversely, if the glider dove because the center of pressure moved behind the center of gravity, the elevator was flexed so that its bottom surface was presented to the wind, forcing the glider upward to a level attitude.

The Wrights' use of a movable elevator to keep pace with the constantly roving center of pressure was a simple but effective solution to controlling the glider in pitch. The elevator has been employed for pitch control on virtually every airplane since.

In addition to being movable, the location of the Wrights' elevator was also unusual. Unlike Pénaud, Lilienthal, Chanute, and others, who mounted their horizontal stabilizing surface behind the wings, the brothers placed theirs in front. A forward elevator, known as a canard, is extremely effective in lessening the violent reaction of a stall. When designing their first glider, the Wrights did not understand stalls. Placing the elevator ahead of the wings was largely an intuitive decision in response to fear of a deadly nosedive like the one that had claimed Lilienthal's life. It worked just as they hoped. Rather than the chilling spin following a stall that was common to aircraft with the elevator in the rear, the Wrights' canard design settled to the ground almost parachute-style. The glider might hit the ground with a thud but usually not hard enough to damage the machine or injure the pilot.

HAVING SORTED THROUGH THE ISSUE OF CENTER OF PRESSURE AND PITCH CONTROL, THE Wrights then tackled the other fundamental aerodynamic problem initially facing them: the curvature of the airfoil. By 1900, the greater aerodynamic efficiency of curved surfaces had been established beyond question. Only the precise shape of the curve was a matter of debate. Lilienthal, Chanute, and others had used a perfect arc with some success in their gliders. The Wrights chose to place the high point of the curve closer to the leading edge of the wing on their glider. They did so because when the wing is near horizontal, less of the surface area of the top side of the wing is exposed to the wind. They hoped that this would limit the downward pressure, which in turn, they believed, contributed to the reversal of the movement of the center of pressure.

The depth of the airfoil's curvature, known as camber, also had to be considered. Lilienthal used a camber of 1 in 12 on his gliders. This means that the chord, or width of the wing, was 12 times the height of the wing at the peak of the curve. The Wrights again departed from standard practice and chose a much shallower camber of 1 in 22. They reasoned that a flatter camber, with the high point ahead of the center of the chord, would aid in limiting the travel of the center of lifting pressure along the surface of the wing and thereby make the aircraft more stable in pitch and easier to control. They argued that with a highly arched wing with the peak of the curve comparatively far back, a great deal of the upper surface of the wing is exposed to the oncoming flow of air when the wing is at or near horizontal. The significant amount of downward pressure that would be generated by so much of the upper surface exposed to the wind, they believed, would cause the center of pressure to reverse abruptly and rapidly move toward the rear, and that would result in a very unstable aircraft. Based on this reasoning, the Wrights postulated that a shallow airfoil with the high point far forward would produce a more gentle reversal of the movement of the center of pressure and thus a more stable aircraft.

The layout of the Wright machine differed in one other significant respect from previous gliders, and that was the position of the pilot. Lilienthal, Chanute, and virtually everyone else making tentative glider flights at this time rode their aircraft slung vertically between the wings. The Wrights, on the other hand, chose to have the pilot lie prone on the bottom wing, as a way to limit drag due to wind resistance. According to their calculations, total drag of their glider was cut in half with the pilot in the horizontal position compared with when the pilot was upright. Interestingly, in order to corroborate their estimates of the surface area exposed to the wind of a pilot lying prone compared with one flying upright, they went through an elaborate analysis of the wind resistance generated by a bicycle rider under known conditions.

Despite the sound engineering reasons for flying prone, most of the brothers' contemporaries felt that the Wrights' gliding position was too dangerous. Octave Chanute, for example, admonished them, even though he agreed with their reasoning: "This is a magnificent showing, provided that you do not plow the ground with your noses." True to form, the brothers did it their way and suffered no ill effects.

With the kite and the glider, the Wrights had worked through several of the more complex aerodynamic problems. They next turned to the obvious question of size. How large a wing area would be required and how light must the craft be in order to lift the weight of a human being into the air? Fortunately, to answer these questions the Wrights were able to draw on their literature search. A number of mathematical relationships had been established for the speed, surface area, lift, and drag needed to successfully fly a craft of a certain size and weight by the time the brothers began their aeronautical research. These relationships had evolved over two centuries largely through intuitive reasoning and experimental analysis in other fields, such as fluid mechanics. They had been published in a contemporary handbook called *Pocket-Book of Aeronautics,* compiled by a German military officer named Hermann W. L. Moedebeck, and in other sources available to the Wrights. Lilienthal had even compiled and published a set of actual lift and drag data for the specific wing shape he used for his gliders, and the Wrights used these as their starting point.

The brothers at last began to design an actual aircraft based on all their careful theoretical planning. Relying on the existing equations and Lilienthal's data, they calculated the appropriate dimensions of their own glider and began construction in mid-August 1900, about a year after they tested their comparatively simple wing-warping kite. In only a few short weeks, the Wrights had prefabricated the majority of the parts for that first glider. Every piece—the ribs, the struts, the metal fittings, even the fine French sateen fabric that would cover the spruce and ash framework—was carefully prepared to allow for simple assembly upon reaching the site of their gliding experiments.

Finally, after much hard work sorting out numerous complex issues, the brothers were ready. They had carefully considered questions regarding control and aerodynamics and had developed imaginative solutions to a range of design problems. They determined the general layout of their glider, calculated how large it had to be, and engineered and fabricated its individual components. The time had come to test their ideas in actual practice. By early September 1900, less than a year and a half after Wilbur Wright had written to the Smithsonian Institution requesting information on the subject of human flight, the Wright brothers were ready to take their first tentative steps into the air.

SETTING OUT AS WE DID, WITH

ALMOST REVOLUTIONARY THEORIES

... AND AN ENTIRELY UNTRIED ...

MACHINE, WE CONSIDERED IT QUITE

A POINT ... TO RETURN WITHOUT

HAVING OUR PET THEORIES

COMPLETELY KNOCKED IN THE HEAD

... AND OUR OWN BRAINS DASHED

OUT IN THE BARGAIN.

Wilbur Wright 1900

3

RIDING
THE WINDS

1900: *The Wright brothers' first full-size glider strains against its tether at Kitty Hawk.*

S WILBUR AND ORVILLE STUDIED basic aerodynamics and began to design their first glider, they decided to write the grand old man of aeronautics, Octave Chanute. They were convinced that their preliminary ideas were sound and that they were ready to consult with someone of Chanute's stature in the aeronautical community. That first contact with America's best known aeronautical experimenter in the spring of 1900 would have a long-term impact on their work and personal lives. It was also important historically because it brought the Wrights into direct communication with a leading figure in aeronautics, and it began a series of detailed letters that to a great extent would trace the story of the invention of the airplane. The initial letter Wilbur sent to Chanute, dated May 13, 1900, was the first of approximately 400 letters they would exchange until Chanute's death in 1910. Though self-effacing and appropriately deferential in his tone, Wilbur was very forthright as he expressed his ideas on the flying problem and how he planned to approach it. It was common for Chanute to correspond with engineers and scientists with international reputations. Nevertheless, he was particularly impressed with the ideas and plans shared by this modest bicycle-shop proprietor from Dayton, Ohio.

He immediately recognized that the writer was no ordinary mechanic. Always eager to lend whatever support he could to promising and enthusiastic young aeronautical experimenters, Chanute quickly penned an encouraging response to Wilbur's letter. A mutual admiration and warm friendship rapidly developed as the letters between the Wrights and Chanute became more frequent.

During the Wrights' experimental years, and for a good while after, many people assumed a greater contribution by Chanute to the brothers' success than was actually the case. Because of his senior years and prominent position in the aeronautical field, it was widely believed that he mentored the Wrights. Despite almost constant communication, this was not so. Throughout the years of their association, Chanute provided the Wrights with little genuine technical assistance and few, if any, useful theoretical ideas—though the influence of the Chanute-Herring "two-surface" glider of 1896 on the Wrights' initial design might be considered an exception. On the contrary, Chanute frequently did not understand the ideas and principles Wilbur and Orville discussed with him, and he typically mischaracterized what the Wrights had done when telling others about it.

Chanute did make a significant contribution as a source of moral support. Particularly at times of difficulty and frustration, Chanute played an important role as confidence builder to Wilbur and Orville. He was always ready and willing to be a sounding board for the Wrights' ideas and proposed solutions, and occasionally he was able to point out errors or suggest the brothers were exercising bad judgment. Chanute's friendly, ever enthusiastic exchanges with the Wrights were a major source of encouragement to them and played no small part in their seeing their projects through to completion. One thing Chanute knew for certain: Wilbur and Orville Wright had done more in the short time they had been at work on human flight than the numerous other young experimenters he had helped and sometimes supported financially. He was going to assist them in any way he could

In that first letter to Chanute, Wilbur discussed his work at great length. He provided a well-written outline of the brothers' research to date and their plans to build and test a full-size, piloted glider. Then, only in the last few sentences, did he finally ask the established leader of pioneer flight research for any advice. Wilbur inquired about suitable locations to fly such a craft. He needed a place with strong, steady winds and open spaces. Without an engine, a glider needs the wind to generate a good steady flow of air over the wing. Open, sandy terrains would allow for relatively safe gliding. Chanute suggested San Diego, California, and St. James City, Florida. He also recommended investigating the Atlantic coasts of South Carolina and Georgia.

The brothers made an inquiry to the federal weather bureau in Washington, D.C., and received publications containing tables of average wind speeds for a variety of places around the country. A number of sites looked promising. The Wrights settled on an isolated strip of beach off the coast of

1900: *The Kitty Hawk post office doubled as the home of postmaster William Tate and his family. Tate was the Wrights' enthusiastic host and also helped with glider launches.*

North Carolina. A place known as Kitty Hawk. Wilbur explained the reasoning behind his choice to his father:

> I chose Kitty Hawk because it seemed the place which most closely met the required conditions. In order to obtain support from the air it is necessary … to move through it at the rate of 15 or 20 miles per hour …. It is safer to practice in a wind, provided this is not too much broken up into eddies and sudden gusts by hills, trees, and so forth. At Kitty Hawk, which is on the narrow bar separating the Sound from the Ocean, there are neither hills nor trees, so that it offers a safe place for practice.

In addition to offering suitable conditions for the glider tests, Kitty Hawk also provided the brothers with a degree of privacy, and it was reasonably accessible from their home, Dayton, Ohio.

THE ORIGIN OF THE NAME KITTY HAWK IS SURROUNDED BY SEVERAL LEGENDS. ONE SUGGESTS that during early English settlement of the area, the name became an anglicized version of "Killy Honk," a local Indian expression for killing the geese that migrated to the area every fall. Another version suggests the name is derived from "skeeter hawk," an insect eater that frequents the area and feeds on the prodigious mosquito population.

The choice of Kitty Hawk was made after the Wrights received two welcoming letters in response to their inquiry to the local weather station on August 3, 1900. The observer at the station, Joseph J. Dosher, after writing his own positive reply, passed on Wilbur's letter to William J. Tate, a local resident who was considered the best educated person in the modest little fishing village. Tate wrote back as well. He enthusiastically endorsed Kitty Hawk as a "fine place" to conduct the "scientific kite flying" experiments the Wrights described. He concluded with an offer of whatever assistance he could provide. "If you decide to try your machine here & come I will take pleasure in doing all I can for your convenience & success & pleasure, & I assure you you will find a hospitable people when you come among us," Tate wrote. Kitty Hawk seemed ideal. The Wrights looked no further and immediately made plans to visit the coastal village with the glider they had painstakingly designed the previous year.

Despite offering everything they were looking for in a test site, Kitty Hawk could be a harsh place. Sudden squalls would frequently blow up off the ocean. Orville described the storms in a letter home to his sister, Katharine:

This is "just before the battle," sister, just before the squall begins. About two or three nights a week we have to crawl up at ten or eleven o'clock to hold the tent down. When one of these 45-mile nor'easters strikes us, you can depend on it, there is little sleep in our camp ….

Orville went on humorously,

We each of us have two blankets, but almost freeze every night. The wind blows in on my head, and I pull the blankets up over my head, when my feet freeze, and I reverse the process. I keep this up all night and in the morning am hardly able to tell "where I'm at" in the bedclothes.

The ubiquitous sand was a definite asset for soft landings, but it could be an inconvenience as it was constantly being blown and sifted about. It found its way into every corner and crevice of the Wrights' living quarters, cots, and clothes. "But the sand!" Orville exclaimed, "The sand is the greatest thing in Kitty Hawk, and soon will be the only thing." Years later he remarked that the place was "like the Sahara, or what I imagine the Sahara to be."

Insects, especially mosquitoes, were a constant annoyance. "They chewed us clear through our underwear and socks," Orville complained. "Lumps began swelling up all over my body like hen's eggs. … Misery! Misery!"

Lack of food in the area was also a frequent problem. The brothers dealt with that by bringing ample provisions of their own.

Despite the hardships, Wilbur and Orville still viewed their trips to Kitty Hawk as vacations. It was a nice break from the routine of city life. They liked being in the outdoors and grew fond of the local residents they came to know. Testing their aeronautical ideas in the field was extremely exhilarating. They would always consider their visits to Kitty Hawk as some of the happiest times of their lives. Above all, the clear, expansive stretches of soft sand, rolling dunes, and hearty breezes made Kitty Hawk an ideal place to do what the Wright brothers went there to do—fly.

Wilbur arrived for the first time at this obscure North Carolina hamlet he and his brother would make famous on September 12, 1900. The shipping crates carrying the glider were delivered soon after. Orville stayed longer in Dayton to take care of some business matters and joined Wilbur a couple of weeks later with their camping equipment, cots, and other provisions. In the meantime, William Tate offered Wilbur a place to stay in his home. By the first week in October both Wrights were in camp and the glider was assembled. They were ready to put their efforts of the past year to the test.

The total wing area of the glider was 165 square feet, resulting from 17-foot-span biplane wings with a 5-foot chord. It weighed 52 pounds without the pilot. The wing ribs were cut from ash strips and steam bent to a camber of approximately 1 in 23. There was only a single layer of the French sateen fabric covering on the glider. The ribs were slipped into pockets that had been sewn into the underside of the covering.

Construction of the craft was distinctive. It did not have a rigid wooden structure with the fabric sewn directly to it, as was the standard approach. The individual components of the airframe were not fastened together. Rather, they merely "floated" inside pockets sewn into the fabric covering. An added ingenious feature of the fabric was that it was applied to the wing structure with the direction of the weave on the bias. This created a stiffness across the frame without hindering wing warping for lateral control. Making the fabric an integral part of the structure in this way also eliminated the need for extra bracing, which saved weight. Also to save weight, no varnish or sealant was applied to the fabric. The area on the lower wing where the pilot would lie was left uncovered.

Like the 1899 kite, the biplane wings of the 1900 glider were trussed with wire lengthwise across the front and rear bays but had no bracing fore and aft, again to allow for wing warping. The prone pilot would operate the forward elevator with levers extending from the rear of the surface to flex it up or down. A foot-operated wooden crossbar with cables leading to the wing tips controlled the wing warping. Control to the right or left was achieved by pushing on the crossbar with the appropriate foot.

The Wrights first flight-tested the glider by flying it as a tethered kite, with lines running to the ground to operate the controls. Most of the time they kited the glider empty or with 50 pounds of chain for ballast, but occasionally one of the brothers would get on board for a tethered flight.

Wilbur and Orville had hoped to log a lot of flying time over the soft sands at Kitty Hawk. They knew that learning to fly their glider would be as demanding as designing and building the craft, and on October 20, they were ready to make their first free glide. They moved four miles down the beach to a series of three large sand dunes known as Kill Devil Hills. Beginning cautiously, at an altitude of no more than a foot, they made their first few tries, each lasting less than 10 seconds. By the end of the day, they were managing to stay aloft between 15 and 20 seconds and were covering 300 to 400 feet. Most impressive was the ease and precision with which Wilbur was able to control the pitch of the glider. It was nothing like the violent, acrobatic movements required by having to shift body weight for control. He was able to lie still on his craft and deftly command its flight path with hand and mind working in precise unison. Wilbur made all the free glides in 1900, logging a total of two minutes in the air in the course of a dozen flights.

The Wrights' plans to spend long periods in the air learning to pilot their glider proved to be overly optimistic. Their first season at Kitty Hawk was disappointing in that respect. Nevertheless, the basic effectiveness of their wing-warping system was confirmed, and their belief that the movable forward elevator would help limit the travel of the center of pressure and enable to pilot to control the aircraft

1901: *The Wrights greatly increased their second glider's wing area—to 290 square feet—but its performance was still poor.*

The brothers returned to Dayton greatly discouraged.

"Men would not fly for fifty years," Wilbur reportedly told Orville.

1901: The Wrights' second glider is tested unmanned. The brothers' methodical program of flight-testing always began with kiting the gliders before attempting free glides.

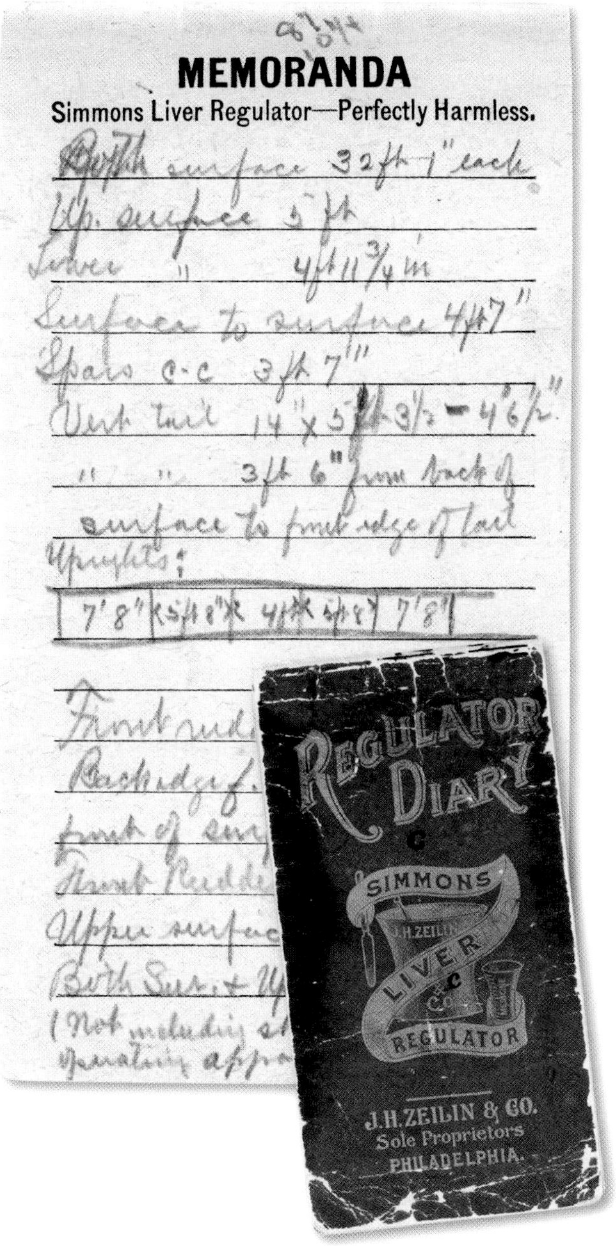

MEMORANDA
Simmons Liver Regulator—Perfectly Harmless.

[handwritten notes:]

Both surface 32 ft 1" each

Up. surface 5 ft

Lower " 4 ft 11¾ in

Surface to surface 4 ft 7"

Spars c·c 3 ft 7"

Vert tail 14" x 5 ft 3½ — 4'6½"

" " 3 ft 6" from back of

surface to front edge of tail

Uprights:

7'8" 5'8" 4' 4'8" 7'8"

Front rud...

Back edge...

front of sur...

Front Rudder...

Upper surfac...

Both Sur. + U...

(Not including ...

operating appa...

[diary cover:] REGULATOR DIARY — SIMMONS J.H. ZEILIN & Co. LIVER REGULATOR — J.H. ZEILIN & CO. Sole Proprietors PHILADELPHIA.

1901: After a successful test flight, the glider makes a soft landing. The Wrights recorded the results of their flights and experiments in small vest-pocket notebooks, like this one written in Orville's hand.

in pitch with great precision was more than fulfilled. They also learned that the structural integrity of their design was sound and that it was easily repaired when damage did occur.

Even though the Wrights were able to come away with these positives, there was a very troubling, and baffling, result: The lift produced by the glider was far less than their calculations predicted. It generated only about half of what it should have. For all their careful planning, something was very wrong.

They retraced their steps to try to see where they might have made a mistake. Maybe they should not have deviated from Lilienthal's flight-tested curvature of 1 in 12, using a flatter camber of 1 in 23. Perhaps not sealing the fabric to make it airtight reduced the lift. Then there were the aerodynamic data and the lift and drag equations the Wrights had used. The poor aerodynamic performance of the glider raised serious doubts about the accepted equations and Lilienthal's lift data.

The lift problem notwithstanding, the Wrights still were quite satisfied with their first experiments in the field. They validated a number of their ideas about control and structural design, the flight trials had proved to be relatively safe, and their stay at Kitty Hawk was pleasant and invigorating. Nor was it a financial risk; the 1900 glider cost them a mere $15 to build. All things considered, they saw no reason not to continue their aeronautical work and made plans to return to the little fishing village with a new glider the following year. Wilbur later summed it up:

> We were very much pleased with the general results of the trip, for setting out as we did, with almost revolutionary theories on many points, and an entirely untried form of machine, we considered it quite a point to be able to return without having our pet theories completely knocked in the head by the hard logic of experience, and our own brains dashed out in the bargain.

IN SPITE OF THEIR SUSPICIONS ABOUT THE DATA AND EQUATIONS THEY HAD USED TO DESIGN THE 1900 glider, the Wrights were still not ready to toss them aside. After all, this was the work of the established leaders in the field. Who were they to reject it, the brothers modestly believed. On their next craft, they would simply increase the size of the wings to improve the lift.

Again a biplane, the 1901 glider had a 22-foot wingspan and a 7-foot chord, giving it a net wing area of 290 square feet, after making the opening for the pilot in the lower wing. It weighed 98 pounds unloaded. Beyond the significant increase in wing area, they tried increasing the camber to Lilienthal's proven 1 in 12 as a further measure to remedy the lift deficiency. This seemed reasonable given that the

Lilienthal data were derived from a 1 in 12 airfoil. Not to be locked into this change, however, the Wrights cleverly constructed their new glider so that the camber could be altered during their experiments in the field.

The Wrights were back at Kitty Hawk in July 1901. In addition to their tent, this year they erected a rough 16 x 25-foot hangar to store the new, larger glider. With delays because of the rain, the week required to build the hangar, and time spent assembling the glider, it was not until July 27 that the Wrights were ready to resume the exciting gliding experiments they had begun the previous fall.

Wilbur got off to a good start on the first day, making 17 free glides, a few covering more than 300 feet. The performance impressed the few helpers and observers who were on hand, but the Wrights were discouraged. Despite the increased wing area, there was no improvement in lift. More disconcerting, the pitch control on the new glider was not as solid and responsive as it had been on the 1900 craft. In nearly every critical area, the new glider did not live up to expectations.

The brothers took advantage of their foresight in designing the glider so the camber could be adjusted and retrussed the wings to a flatter airfoil of 1 in 19, closer to what it had been in 1900. This immediately solved the problem. The responsive action of the forward elevator returned, allowing Wilbur to follow the undulating contour of the terrain with amazing ease and precision. His two best glides after the change covered 366 and 389 feet.

Feeling more confident after curing the pitch-control problem, Wilbur took the next step and attempted to make an intentional turn with wing warping. So far the wing warping had worked flawlessly, but this time, when Wilbur warped the wings to make a real turn, a startling thing happened. He started a turn to the left, which began normally, but then the glider reversed direction on its own and began to turn back to the right. Taken aback by this odd reaction, Wilbur quickly straightened out and landed. Another try produced the same result. They had no idea what was going on and were quite frustrated, having just struggled to get the pitch control back in order.

It had been a very discouraging several weeks for Wilbur and Orville. True, they had made more glides than in 1900, but now they had even more questions and doubts. They had made no headway on the mystery of the dismal lift performance of the glider, and now the curious behavior of their heretofore reliable wing-warping system raised a raft of new, unexplored problems. To date, the 1901 aircraft was the largest glider ever flown. But that was small consolation to the Wrights. Such an achievement held little meaning if it did not lead to resolving the fundamental problems of mechanical flight. They were not interested in isolated records. Their goal was a true airplane.

This was clearly the low point in the brothers' path to the invention of the airplane. In 1908, when recalling this disconsolate period in their experimental work, Wilbur admitted that on the trip

1902: *With Wilbur piloting, Orville and Dan Tate launch the brothers' most successful glider into the air on October 18 at Kitty Hawk.*

FOLLOWING PAGES | 1902: *A movable vertical tail solves the persistent lateral-control problem. The brothers made hundreds of controlled glides in this craft and finally felt ready to build a powered airplane.*

back to Dayton, he had told Orville dejectedly "that men would not fly for fifty years." In the 1940s, when Orville shared the story with Wright biographer Fred Kelly, the statement was emboldened to "not within a thousand years would man ever fly!" Wilbur may or may not have actually uttered those words, but they no doubt reflected the disheartened mood that overtook the brothers as they headed home from Kitty Hawk in August 1901. For the moment, at least, Wilbur and Orville were more than happy to get back to their bicycles.

FORTUNATELY, ENTHUSIASM FOR THEIR EXPERIMENTS QUICKLY RESUMED AFTER THE BROTHERS returned to Dayton. Not two weeks after they were back in the house, their sister, Katharine, lamented to their father, "We don't hear anything but flying machine and engine from morning till night."

Some new shop equipment helped brighten the brothers' spirits. They bought a drill press and band saw, along with overhead line shafting and belts to operate them. They built a small one-cylinder engine fueled by illuminating gas to drive the new machinery. It was crude, but it worked. These additions to their shop enabled the Wrights to make aircraft parts of increasing complexity and facilitated their bicycle manufacture.

The Wrights' flagging interest in flying was also rekindled in their home darkroom. As they developed the pictures they took at Kitty Hawk, they relived the exhilaration of skimming over the sand on board their man-made wings.

> The excitement of gliding experiments does not entirely cease with the breaking up of camp. In the photographic darkroom at home we pass moments of as thrilling interest as any in the field, when the image begins to appear on the plate and it is yet an open question whether we have a picture of a flying machine, or merely a patch of open sky.

Any thoughts of abandoning their aeronautical experiments were finally erased when Wilbur received an invitation from Octave Chanute to speak in Chicago before the prestigious Western Society of Engineers on the brothers' recent gliding experiments at Kitty Hawk. Though flattered by the invitation, Wilbur had never spoken publicly on aeronautics and was apprehensive about presenting a lecture to a group of professional engineers.

The Wrights built a wind tunnel in late 1901 (top) to collect more reliable aerodynamic data. Model wing surfaces (left) were mounted on the upper tier of the lift balance (right), and the lift generated by the model wing was balanced against the pressure on the four resistance fingers attached on the lower tier.

With the encouragement of Orville and Katharine, Wilbur graciously accepted the opportunity with a self-effacing reply to Chanute, agreeing to deliver a "brief paper of rather informal nature" at the society's upcoming meeting in September. As the date of Wilbur's talk approached, his brother and sister asked him whether the speech was going to be witty or scientific. Wilbur quipped he thought it would be "pathetic."

He boarded an early morning train on the day of the speech, September 18. Orville did not join him but contributed the shirt, cuffs, cuff links, and overcoat that Wilbur wore. Orville was far more fastidious than Wilbur. Family members frequently commented on his dapper, tidy appearance, even after a day in the workshop. The Wrights' favorite niece, Ivonette, later recalled, "I don't believe there ever was a man who could do the work he did in all kinds of dirt, oil and grime and come out of it looking immaculate .… when the job was finished he'd come out looking like he was right out of a band box." Wilbur, on the other hand, although always suitably dressed, did not pay great attention to matters of style and fit. Katharine often had to offer a kind reminder that his suit needed pressing or something did not match. On the morning of the Western Society of Engineers speech, however, he was in no need of assistance. Katharine remarked in a letter to their father, "We discovered that to some extent 'clothes do make the man' for you never saw Will look so 'swell.'"

Wilbur's lecture to Chanute's colleagues and associates was anything but "pathetic." As he spoke about the design and construction of the 1900 and 1901 gliders and the brothers' experiences at Kitty Hawk, Wilbur outlined the fundamental aerodynamic and control concepts he and Orville had developed since 1899 and what they had learned from testing them in actual flight trials. In particularly clear and precise terms, he discussed the importance of control, wing warping, the movement and reversal of the center of pressure, the stall characteristics of the forward elevator, and the necessity of acquiring piloting skill. Wilbur complemented the talk with lantern slides of the Wrights' gliders, as well as those of other experimenters' aircraft. It was a remarkably concise and insightful statement of the problem of flight as it stood in the fall of 1901.

Those in attendance were quite impressed with Wilbur's presentation. When the society published a transcript of it in its proceedings, it was read by virtually everyone in the aeronautical community. Abstracts and reprints appeared in scientific and engineering journals all over the U.S. and Europe. The clearly written, thoughtful paper, modestly entitled "Some Aeronautical Experiments," became a benchmark in pioneering aeronautical literature, supplanting *Progress in Flying Machines* and the *Aeronautical Annuals* as the most up-to-date source of information in the field.

This opportunity to share their thinking on aeronautics publicly was helpful to the Wrights at a critical time in their path to the airplane. To have been invited to speak before experienced engineering professionals by such a well-known figure as Octave Chanute did much to confirm in their own minds that they were making significant progress, even with the recent disappointments at Kitty Hawk. The event legitimized their position in the aeronautical community and gave them the confidence to continue with their own ideas, even if they ran counter to the prevailing wisdom of established experimenters.

When the Wrights returned to Dayton after the 1901 gliding experiments, they were convinced that their earlier suspicions about the accuracy of the previously published aerodynamic data and equations were warranted. Wilbur informed Chanute on September 26, 1901, that he was "arranging to make a positive test of the correctness of Lilienthal's coefficients." In October 1901, the Wrights began a series of tests to check the values in Lilienthal's table of aerodynamic data. The values in question related to the coefficients of lift and drag. The coefficient of lift is the term in the lift equation that relates the specific angle of the wing in relation to the oncoming flow of air (called angle of attack) to the force of lift generated by the wing. After designing two poorly performing gliders using coefficients directly from Lilienthal's table, the Wrights were now inclined to think these values might be flawed.

Another critical term in the lift equation was Smeaton's coefficient. Developed in the 18th century, this constant of proportionality was used in the relationship between pressure and velocity when studying bodies in a flow. It accounts for the density of the medium through which the body is moving. In the case of an airplane wing, the medium is of course air. A value of 0.005 had been established for air, and the Wrights had used it in designing their first two gliders. An error in this constant would have provided another explanation for the less-than-expected lift of the gliders—even apart from any inaccuracy of Lilienthal's lift coefficients. The Wrights were also regarding Smeaton's coefficient with increasing uncertainty.

After making some preliminary measurements with makeshift testing devices, the Wrights decided to build a wind tunnel to generate their own set of coefficients of lift and drag and compare them with Lilienthal's.

THE WRIGHTS WERE NOT THE FIRST TO USE A WIND TUNNEL. BEGINNING WITH THE instrument produced by Francis Wenham and John Browning in 1871, approximately a dozen wind tunnels were experimented with during the last quarter of the 19th century. But the way in which the brothers used their wind tunnel in 1901 differed from previous instruments in a very important way. They were the first to collect systematically specific data on a wide range of prospective wing shapes and use them in conjunction with the established lift and drag equations. No one before had used a wind tunnel to gather aerodynamic data in a form that could be incorporated directly into the design of an actual aircraft. Theirs was a well-designed apparatus and produced accurate results, but aside from the technical superiority of the Wright tunnel, the manner in which the brothers used it made it so much more effective than anything that had preceded it.

The Wright wind tunnel was a simple wooden box 6 feet long and 16 inches square, with a glass window on top for viewing the interior during testing. A fan belted off the overhead line shafting run by their one-horsepower shop engine provided the airflow, generating a wind of approximately 30 miles per hour. The data were collected using small model wing surfaces about 6 square inches in area, cut from sheet metal.

What really set the Wright wind tunnel apart were the test instruments that the little model wings were mounted on. The brothers called them balances because they operated on the principle of balancing the lift of a model wing surface against an opposing force in order to evaluate the surface's lift and drag properties over a range of angles of attack. The Wrights designed the balances to represent physically what the lift and drag equations expressed mathematically. In other words, they were designed to measure values related to the actual aerodynamic forces acting on the model surface in terms that could be substituted directly into the equations. It was a brilliant intuitive leap. There were two separate balances, one for measuring lift and one for drag. Made of old hacksaw blades and bicycle spokes, the instruments had a crude appearance that belied their sophistication.

Using readings from the balances in the wind tunnel, along with the actual measurements of lift, drag, and velocity yielded by the trials of the full-size gliders at Kitty Hawk, the Wrights ultimately were able to derive values experimentally for each of the variables and constants in the equations. This allowed them not only to check Lilienthal's data and Smeaton's coefficient independently but also to generate their own table of lift coefficients, which in turn enabled them to build an aircraft that would perform in accordance with prior calculations. The brothers' artful interweaving of their clear, straightforward conceptualization of the problem and their clever, effective means of experimentally obtaining results illustrates the Wrights' engineering talents at their finest.

During October and November 1901 the Wrights gathered data on more than 200 different wing curvatures and shapes. The Lilienthal table contained data for only one, his 1 in 12, perfect-arc wing profile. Wilbur and Orville now had lift and drag coefficients for a vast array of wings. Using this impressive set of data, the Wrights determined that not only were Lilienthal's coefficients probably off, but that the time-honored value for Smeaton's coefficient was 40 percent too high. The Wrights corrected it to 0.0033.

The gathering of accurate lift and drag coefficients was the central purpose of the wind tunnel research, but the Wrights also investigated other significant aerodynamic properties of curved wing surfaces with the tunnel. Aspect ratio—the ratio of the length of the wing to its width—was extremely important to aircraft design. The wind tunnel experiments showed the brothers that long, narrow wings are more efficient than short, wide ones with the same area. The wings of the Wrights' third glider, built in 1902, had this more favorable layout and produced far greater lift than their 1901 glider, with only a slight increase in wing area.

They also performed wind tunnel tests on the thickness and shape of the wing's leading edge and the ways in which varying the gap between biplane and triplane wing arrangements affected performance. When they began designing their first powered airplane in 1903, the Wrights again used their wind tunnel to test the drag properties of different cross-sectional contours for the vertical wing struts.

WILBUR AND ORVILLE WERE FASCINATED BY THE AERODYNAMIC RESEARCH THEY WERE conducting, but by mid-December 1901, they realized that they had to set it aside. Earlier in the year, they had hired an assistant to help out with the bicycle shop named Charlie Taylor. While they had been closeted away, immersed in their aeronautical work, Charlie had managed the shop. As much as the Wrights cherished the opportunity to focus on intellectual pursuits, the bicycle business was their livelihood, and they knew they could no longer neglect their responsibilities. "The boys have finished … their experiments. As soon as the results are put into tables, they will begin work for next season's bicycles," Katharine reported to their father.

Octave Chanute had been following the brothers' wind tunnel experiments with great interest, even helping to put the data into charts and tables. He was disappointed to see them stop and offered to use his connections to fund their experiments. "I happen to know Carnegie," Chanute informed Wilbur and Orville. "Would you like for me to write to him?" Not wanting to be beholden to anyone, the Wrights preferred to conduct their investigations from the profits of their own business. Wilbur diffused the matter with a tongue-in-cheek response to Chanute's inquiry. "A salary of ten or twenty thousand a year would be no insuperable objection, but I think it possible that Andrew is too hardheaded a Scotchman to become interested in such a visionary pursuit as flying."

A critical turning point in the path to mechanical flight, the 1901 wind tunnel experiments provided

1902: *In September Orville finally made his first free glides. Here, Wilbur and Dan Tate help him into the air.*

1902: *Wilbur glides above the sands of Kitty Hawk in sustained level flight. By the end of the 1902 season, most of the crucial breakthroughs to flight had been achieved. All that remained was to supply power.*

the body of aerodynamic data that would become the basis of the brothers' first successful airplane. The data were notable for their technical significance and for the speed with which they had been compiled.

The Wright brothers' invention of the airplane was characterized by numerous such intellectual and technical achievements. Linked together, they ultimately produced a complete technological system capable of flight. Independent discoveries, no matter how revolutionary, rarely result in a new invention. It is only when such discoveries are integrated with other discoveries and technical knowledge that practical innovations typically come about. What made the Wright brothers special was that they understood and defined their inventive method in these terms, and they had the talent to follow through on an entire set of problems presented by the creation of a complex mechanical device and arrive at sound solutions.

The Wrights built their third glider in 1902, using the reliable aerodynamic data collected with their own wind tunnel. They chose a very shallow wing curvature and designed the glider such that it could be rigged with varying cambers, from 1 in 24 to 1 in 30. The wind tunnel research on aspect ratio led them to increase the span of the wings to 32 feet, with only a slight increase in overall wing area. The resulting longer, narrower wings gave the 1902 glider a much more elegant appearance than its two predecessors. The foot-operated, wing-warping control in 1900 was difficult to use, so the Wrights tried a different setup on the new glider. The warping cables were connected to a laterally sliding hip cradle mounted at the center of the lower wing, which the pilot actuated by shifting his hips. This was a far more natural movement than the awkward pressing of the feet to make a turn.

The Wrights began testing the new glider at Kitty Hawk in late August 1902. Curious about the efficiency of the new wings based on their own coefficients of lift and drag, they first flew the individual wing surfaces as kites. The results were very encouraging. "We have done a little experimenting with the finished surface and find that it lifts much better than our last year's surface and also has less drift …. it 'soared' on a slope of 7¾°, that is the cords attached to it were vertical."

The kiting tests also suggested that the finished glider probably would have good stability in pitch. "We find one thing about our new surface that is very fortunate. The center of pressure does not reverse till a very low angle [of attack]." The 1900 and modified 1901 gliders exhibited this characteristic and had smooth elevator control response.

As a research technique, the importance of flying the gliders as kites cannot be overemphasized. The 1899 kite was, of course, a comparatively simple and inexpensive means for the Wrights to develop and test their wing-warping control system—one of the most fundamental aspects of their invention. But flying the man-carrying aircraft as kites also provided the brothers with important information that they used to evaluate and improve the design. Measuring angles of attack in flight and tracking the all-important movement of the center of pressure was key to accurately determining the efficiency of the aerodynamics of the aircraft. Kiting enabled them to do that precisely and accurately. As Wilbur put it, "Testing a gliding machine as a kite on a suitable slope … is one of the most satisfactory methods of determining its efficiency." The technique also allowed the brothers to test the response of the control system on the full-size aircraft from the ground in safety. Finally, kiting the gliders with a pilot aboard offered the Wrights a valuable opportunity to get the feel of the aircraft in the air, before attempting free flight.

Wilbur and Orville always returned to kiting to make the initial flight tests of each new glider or to analyze puzzling results observed in free glides. Kiting allowed them to evaluate their theories and experimental data under actual flight conditions for extended periods of time. By providing some sense of the aircraft's flight characteristics, it also tempered the risks of launching oneself off a hill in a completely untried aircraft.

THE FIRST FREE GLIDES OF THE 1902 GLIDER WERE MADE ON SEPTEMBER 20, AND THE improved performance of the new wing shape and curvature were immediately apparent. The 1902 glider's wing area was only 15 square feet greater than the 1901 craft, but it generated much more lift. Equally satisfying, the new glider flew in accordance with calculated performance, confirming the accuracy of the new aerodynamic data and the corrected Smeaton's coefficient.

The 1902 glider differed from its predecessors in another important respect. To deal with the problem of the glider reversing direction in a turn, which Wilbur had faced in 1901, the Wrights added a fixed vertical tail. It eliminated control reversal under certain conditions, but even with this tail the glider had a tendency to stall and spin, if the pilot banked too sharply. The Wrights solved this defect in the control system by converting the fixed tail into a movable rudder, which operated in unison with the wing warping. The glider was now fully, and safely, maneuverable in all three axes of motion. "When properly applied," Wilbur reported, "the means of control proved to possess a mastery over the forces tending to disturb equilibrium."

The Wrights left Kitty Hawk on October 28, full of confidence and enthusiasm. They were able to make sustained flights with the new glider routinely, finally realizing their initial plans to spend a good deal of time in the air learning to fly. They made more than 700 glides in 1902. Wilbur had made all the free glides in 1900 and 1901. This year Orville also shared in the thrill of free flight and began to work on his piloting skills. By the end of their stay at Kitty Hawk that year, flights of 500 feet were common, and a few topped 600 feet. Wilbur could not have been more pleased with the results:

> Our new machine is a very great improvement over anything we had built before and over anything anyone has built …. Yesterday I tried three glides from the top of the hill and made 506 ft., 504½ ft. and 550 ft. respectively …. Everything is so much more satisfactory that we now believe that the flying problem is really nearing its solution.

The wind tunnel experiments performed by the Wrights in late 1901, and their practical application in the 1902 glider, carried the progress toward mechanical flight to another new plateau. In many respects, this phase of the Wrights' work stands as the technological and psychological turning point in their path to the airplane. From their investigation of model wings, they overcame what had been the central stumbling block up to that point, the inefficiency of their lifting surface. The later powered airplane that carried a human being aloft on December 17, 1903, was the product of a thoughtful and precise program of engineering, the heart of which was the wind tunnel.

In many ways, the flight of the Wright brothers' 1902 glider in its final form marked the invention of the airplane. Of course, for sustained, powered flight, an adequate propulsion system beyond mere gravity and the wind had to be developed. But in terms of the fundamental aerodynamic, control, and structural requirements, the 1902 glider represented the resolution of the problem of mechanical flight. In every meaningful sense, it flew just as a Boeing 747 airliner or modern jet fighter flies, and it was the first flying machine ever to do so.

Many difficult tasks remained before the brothers would be winging their way effortlessly through the sky in a powered flying machine. Indeed, the Wrights had to build two aircraft beyond their first successful powered machine of 1903 before finally accomplishing that reality in 1905. However, despite the considerable amount of labor that still lay ahead, these later aircraft were in large measure only refined versions of the basic 1902 design. There was little about them, or the manner in which the Wrights developed them, that paralleled the truly original breakthroughs of the earlier period. These later achievements were of a different character than the initial design stages of the gliders, the wind tunnel experiments, or the perfection of the control system. By late 1902 the creative and original aspects of the Wright brothers' inventive work, with the notable exception of the propellers, were largely completed.

A PICTURE GALLERY

THE
KITTY HAWK
YEARS

Men from the Kill Devil Hills Life Saving Station helped the Wright brothers, who camped nearby on the desolate beach (opposite).

IN THE FALL OF 1900, THE WRIGHT BROTHERS MADE THEIR FIRST TRIP to KITTY Hawk, a remote fishing village at the northern end of North Carolina's Outer Banks. "We located on the bar which separates Albemarle Sound from the ocean," Wilbur wrote. Setting up camp near three large dunes known as Kill Devil Hills, they began testing their aeronautical theories, returning each fall for the next three years. On December 17, 1903, when the brothers took to the air here, these desolate, windswept sands became forever part of history. In 1908 and again in 1911, Kitty Hawk was the scene of more Wright experiments. Though the brothers were plagued by the area's abundant sand and insects, they developed a lasting affection for Kitty Hawk and its helpful residents, simple people "satisfied with what they have."

At the time the airplane flew, the completed propulsion system, including propellers and transmission system, added up to about 200 pounds, exactly what they had planned.

The other essential component of the propulsion system was the propeller, which would transform the power from the engine into the 90 pounds of thrust needed to get off the ground. As they did with each aspect of the project, the Wrights first researched previous work on the subject. They assumed that given decades of marine use, propellers were well understood and that they could simply adapt known theories to aircraft propulsion. The brothers were surprised to learn, however, that no usable theory of operation had been developed for marine propellers.

They ended up spending months thinking, experimenting, and discussing the problem before they decided how to proceed. The breakthrough came when they realized that a propeller could be understood as a rotary wing. They reasoned that the same physics generating an upward-lifting force when a curved wing surface was placed in an airstream would also produce a horizontally oriented thrust when such a surface was positioned vertically and rotated to create the airflow. The Wright propeller would generate thrust aerodynamically, which was fundamentally different from the way a marine propeller worked. A ship advances as its propeller displaces a volume of the water through which it is passing. Orville later recalled their thinking:

> It was apparent that a propeller was simply an aeroplane [a wing] traveling in a spiral course. As we could calculate the effect of an aeroplane [a wing] traveling in a straight course, why should we not be able to calculate the effect of one traveling in a spiral course?

Using this idea, the Wrights could treat the design of the propeller as they did their wings. Yet again, the fruitful wind tunnel research came into play. They could return to the aerodynamic data gathered for wings to select an appropriate airfoil for the blades of their propeller. Now the brothers could confidently create an efficient aerial propeller.

Since there are more variables involved in determining the efficiency of a rotating wing that would be moving forward than with a fixed lifting surface moving through a flow, the design phase of making the propeller was quite complicated. It took some time, but by June 1903, the Wrights had designed and built a pair of highly efficient propellers that were based entirely on a well-conceived theory of operation and thorough calculation. In a letter to a friend and fellow experimenter, Orville shared the latest developments with a clever turn of phrase that succinctly illustrates the brothers' typical method of approaching a problem, as well as their burgeoning self-confidence about eventual success.

> We had been unable to find anything of value in any of the works to which we had access, so that we worked out a theory of our own on the subject, and soon discovered, as we usually do,

that all the propellers built heretofore are all wrong, and then built a pair of propellers … based on our theory, which are all right! (till we have a chance to test them down at Kitty Hawk and find out differently). Isn't it astonishing that all these secrets have been preserved for so many years just so that we could discover them!!"

There were two propellers on the Wrights' powered airplane, each 8½ feet in length. The tips were covered with fabric and varnished to prevent splitting. The Wrights mounted them behind the wings to avoid any unwanted turbulence in the airflow over the wings. The transmission linkage connecting the engine and the propellers consisted of an arrangement of sprockets and chains running from the engine crankshaft to a pair of steel-tube propeller shafts mounted to each side of the aircraft's center section.

The development of the propulsion system is again illustrative of the Wright brothers' fruitful inventive method. Their conceiving of the propeller as a rotary wing is perhaps the best example of the role of visual thinking in the Wrights' creative process. One literally has to "see" the propeller as a wing moving in a spiral course to make this intellectual leap. Even the Wrights' own language—"It was apparent that a propeller was simply an aeroplane traveling in a spiral course"—suggests that this was in fact an encompassing visual realization.

The preliminary literature search, strict engineering technique, and thorough calculation employed to create the propellers also are reflective of how the brothers tackled each problem they faced. Understanding technological systems and technology transfer were at the heart of the design of the Wrights' means of propulsion as well. They readily saw the relationship between estimating horsepower and thrust and cleverly linked the two mechanically by adapting the sprocket-and-chain drive transmission system in common use at the time. And, of course, the sprocket-and-chain transmission was certainly the most visible, though not the most important, manifestation of the bicycle on the Wright *Flyer*.

By midsummer 1903, Wilbur and Orville had completed the design phase of their powered airplane, built the engine and propellers, and were busy fabricating the airframe. They stayed with the forward-elevator canard biplane design that had served them so well with the gliders. A wingspan of 40 feet 4 inches with a 6-foot-2-inch chord gave the finished *Flyer* a wing area of 510 square feet, 10 more than they had anticipated originally. The 1902 glider flew beautifully with a wing camber of close to 1 in 30, but the Wrights increased it to 1 in 20 on the powered airplane, because they felt a deeper curvature would provide better lift for the larger, heavier *Flyer*.

As with the 1902 glider, the controls consisted of a hip cradle, now padded, to operate the wing warping and coupled movable rear rudder, and a simple wooden lever in the pilot's left hand for the elevator. Mounted on a strut next to the pilot was a small complement of instruments to record flight data: An anemometer was calibrated to display in meters the distance the airplane traveled through the air and a stopwatch was on hand to measure the duration of the flights. A revolution counter mounted at the base of the engine crankshaft recorded engine and propeller rpm.

I N WHAT WAS BECOMING AN ANNUAL LATE SUMMER, EARLY FALL RITUAL, PREPARATIONS FOR THE TREK to Kitty Hawk began in September 1903. Wilbur and Orville had approached each of the previous trips as stimulating opportunities to experiment in an exciting new field, as well as a welcome chance to get away from their daily routine and relax for a while. Up to now, their modest goal was to contribute something useful to the field of aeronautics, and have some fun in the process. By by 1903, they hoped to do far more than merely add to the growing body of information on human flight; they were going to fly an airplane.

The Wrights spent three months in Kitty Hawk in 1903, and during that time their spirits and confidence followed an unsettling course of ups and downs. The weather was often bad, and numerous unexpected technical problems arose with the *Flyer*. At times, Wilbur and Orville were not so sure they would fly in 1903. As the results of their efforts alternated between problems and progress, the Wrights used the metaphor of the ups and downs of the stock market to chart their own headway and attitude in the messages they sent home.

> Flying machine market has been very unsteady the past two days. Opened yesterday morning at about 208 (100% means even chance of success) but by noon had dropped to 110. These fluctuations would have produced a panic, I think, in Wall Street, but in this quiet place it only put us to thinking and figuring a little. It gradually improved during rest of yesterday and today and is now almost back to its old mark.

The *Flyer* was too large to put together completely in the bicycle shop in Dayton, so the first time it was entirely assembled was at Kitty Hawk. The Wrights were unnerved to learn that its finished weight had risen to approximately 750 pounds, including the pilot. The engine's extra four horsepower over their minimum design estimate would help, but would it be enough? Orville's diary entry reflected their concern: "After figuring a while, stock in flying machine began dropping rapidly till it was worth very little!"

1903: *Three days before ultimate success, Wilbur makes his first attempt at powered flight. Unfamiliar with the sensitive elevator control, he stalls on takeoff, slightly damaging the forward elevator as the* Flyer *plows into the ground.*

PAGES 124-25 | *The moment of triumph, December 17, 1903: The* Flyer *lifts off its launching rail with Orville piloting and Wilbur running alongside.*

PAGES 126-27 | *On its fourth and final flight, the* Flyer *stays aloft 59 seconds and travels 852 feet—an unprecedented aerial achievement.*

The high weight of the *Flyer* was only the first of their problems. Misfiring of the engine and vibration placed enormous strains on the propeller shafts and also caused the sprockets to continually loosen. During initial run-ups of the engine, the jerking caused by the unsteady rotation of the propellers twisted the shafts and ripped them from their mountings.

The brothers replaced the damaged propeller shafts and tried again. The engine still ran rough, and the vibration caused the sprockets to loosen immediately. No amount of tightening would keep them in place while the engine was running, frustrating the brothers to no end. Finally, though, the problem was solved with a little bicycle-tire cement on the sprocket nuts.

It had taken weeks but at last the engine and transmission system seemed to be in order. Things looked to be turning in the Wrights' favor. In addition to solving the problems with the propulsion system, the higher than expected weight of the *Flyer* no longer troubled the brothers after they measured the thrust delivered by their propellers—132 pounds, 50 percent more than the 90 pounds they had estimated. With both of their major technical problems overcome, the Wrights' confidence soared. "Stock went up like a sky rocket, and is now at the highest figure in history," Orville wrote home enthusiastically. "We will not be ready for trial for several days yet on account of having decided on some changes to the machine. Unless something breaks in the meantime we feel confident of success." By the second week in December, the Wrights were, at last, prepared to make an attempt at powered flight.

The gliders were light enough to be hand–launched with an assistant at each wing tip, but that was not possible with the much larger and heavier *Flyer*. The Wrights built a simple 60-foot launching rail out of four two-by-fours laid end to end. The airplane traveled down the rail on a small, wheeled dolly, or "truck," as the Wrights called it. They jokingly dubbed the launching track the "Grand Junction Railroad."

On December 14, all was ready for the first attempt to fly. With the help of several Kitty Hawk locals who were on hand to witness the trial, the *Flyer* was positioned on the launching rail and the engine warmed up. The honor of making the first flight was determined by the toss of a coin. Wilbur won and then climbed into the hip cradle, while Orville made a last-minute adjustment to the engine. The moment had come.

The restraining line was released and the *Flyer* trundled slowly down the launching rail. After about 40 feet, it lurched into the air sharply, stalled, settled backward, and smashed into the sand on the left wing. The forward elevator was damaged and one of the landing skids broken. The elevator was much more sensitive than what Wilbur was used to in the 1902 glider, causing him to overcontrol the airplane on takeoff. He emerged from the rough landing unscathed.

WHEN WE GOT UP A WIND OF BETWEEN 20 AND 25

MILES WAS BLOWING FROM THE NORTH. WE GOT THE

MACHINE OUT EARLY AND PUT OUT THE SIGNAL FOR

THE MEN AT THE STATION .... AFTER RUNNING THE

ENGINE AND PROPELLERS A FEW MINUTES TO GET

THEM IN WORKING ORDER, I GOT ON THE MACHINE

AT 10:35 FOR THE FIRST TRIAL ....

THE MACHINE LIFTED FROM THE TRUCK JUST AS IT

WAS ENTERING ON THE FOURTH RAIL .... I FOUND

THE CONTROL OF THE FRONT RUDDER QUITE

DIFFICULT .... AS A RESULT THE MACHINE

WOULD RISE SUDDENLY ... THEN AS SUDDENLY ...

DART FOR THE GROUND.

From the diary (left) of Orville Wright, December 17, 1903

The Wrights did not consider Wilbur's first erratic ride a true flight; it had lasted a mere three and a half seconds. But they were more confident than ever now. The engine and propellers performed well and delivered adequate thrust. The controls were responsive, and the airframe survived the hard meeting with the ground with minimal damage. "There is now no question of final success," Wilbur wrote home. Orville echoed the prediction in a telegram he sent to his father the following day.

Misjudgment at start reduced flight to hundred and twelve. Power and control ample. Rudder only injured. Success assured. Keep quiet.

The airplane was repaired and ready for another attempt on the morning of December 17. Freezing temperatures and a 27-mile-per-hour wind greeted the brothers as they moved the *Flyer* out of the hangar. Conditions were far from ideal, but they were running out of time as the harsh Kitty Hawk winter was descending quickly. This was probably their last chance to fly in 1903, and, after coming so close three days before, they did not want to leave Kitty Hawk without a flight. By 10:30 a.m. every-thing was ready and the engine was started. As it warmed up, Wilbur and Orville shared some final words and shook hands. A witness later recalled the scene, saying that "we couldn't help notice how they held on to each other's hand, sort o'like they hated to let go; like two folks parting who weren't sure they'd ever see each other again."

This time it was Orville in the pilot's position, as Wilbur steadied the *Flyer* at the right wing tip. Before getting in the airplane, Orville set up his camera and carefully aimed it at the end of the launch-ing rail. He instructed a local resident named John Daniels about how to snap the shutter and told him to do so the instant the *Flyer* left the rail.

At 10:35 a.m. the *Flyer* began to move slowly forward into the brisk wind. The speed over the ground was only 7 or 8 miles per hour, but airspeed was close to 30 with the wind. As in Wilbur's attempt, the *Flyer* was airborne in a mere 40 feet, and, like Wilbur, Orville had problems managing the sensitive elevator control, causing the airplane to dart up and down as it sailed slowly over the sand. It came to rest with a thud 120 feet from where it had taken off. The brothers had to estimate the time of the flight because the onboard stopwatch zeroed itself when the airplane hit the ground; Wilbur, in his excitement, forgot to start the one he was carrying. They judged the time to be about 12 seconds. It had been a brief and relatively short flight, but a true flight nevertheless.

The Wrights flew the airplane three more times that morning. On the second flight, Wilbur trav-eled 175 feet in a similar up-and-down course. Orville did a little better on the next try, covering slight-ly more than 200 feet in 15 seconds. The last and best flight had Wilbur back at the controls. It began like the others with the *Flyer* pitching up and down. Gaining a little feel for the elevator, Wilbur then managed to smooth out his course and hugged the contour of the beach for several hundred feet before the overly sensitive elevator again caused the airplane to erratically pitch, ending the flight with a dart into the sand. Nevertheless, he had been in the air for 59 seconds and had traveled an impressive 852 feet from the launching rail.

This last, long flight proved without doubt that the Wright brothers had invented the airplane. Without it, skeptics may have called into question the credibility of the relatively short initial flights. No one could deny, however, that the fourth effort was a fully controlled, sustained heavier-than-air flight. Seven years after Lilienthal's fatal crash, four and a half years after Wilbur's eloquent letter to the Smithsonian Institution, the Wright brothers had achieved the timeless dream of human flight.

The elevator was broken slightly in the hard landing of the last flight. As the Wrights were assessing the situation and considering another flight, a strong gust of wind swept past the airplane, overturning it, and sending it tumbling across the sand. The damage was beyond what they could repair in the field. There would be no more flying in 1903, but the Wrights could now leave Kitty Hawk with their goal achieved.

After a break for lunch, Wilbur and Orville walked the four miles from Kill Devil Hills to Kitty Hawk to send a telegram to their father confirming the hopeful message sent 48 hours earlier.

Success four flights thursday morning all against twenty one mile wind   started from Level with engine power alone   average speed through air thirty one miles   longest 57 seconds   inform Press   home Christmas.*

Three weeks after the successful first flights at Kitty Hawk, the Wrights prepared a statement for the Associated Press in response to several wildly exaggerated reports that had appeared shortly after December 17. The brothers provided an accurate account of the events, and then, in closing, affirmed that their primary goal had been achieved: "… packed our goods and returned home, knowing that the age of the flying machine had come at last."

The Wright brothers inaugurated the aerial age with the Kitty Hawk flights of 1903. They were the world's first powered, controlled flights in a heavier-than-air piloted aircraft. But until the airplane was capable of more than short, marginal, straight-line jaunts, it could not be considered a practical invention. Marketing and exploiting the technology would require an aircraft capable of making turns

*The telegram incorrectly stated the duration as 57 rather than 59 seconds. Also, the wind speed given was an average for the morning the flights were made.

1904: *Orville (left) and Wilbur stand before their second powered airplane. After their success at Kitty Hawk, the brothers continued their aeronautical experiments at a cow pasture known as Huffman Prairie, a few miles from Dayton.*

The Aerial Age Begins

and operating over more commonplace terrains than the sandy, open spaces of Kitty Hawk. Like the inventors behind any prototype, the Wrights would have to bring theirs to a level of practical utility if it was going to have broad impact. To do just that, Wilbur and Orville built two more experimental powered airplanes in 1904 and in 1905.

THE JOURNEY TO KITTY HAWK WAS ALWAYS ARDUOUS AND TOOK THE BROTHERS AWAY FROM their business for extended periods, so they decided to find a site closer to home to continue their flying experiments. Huffman Prairie, a local cow pasture eight miles outside Dayton, served their needs. The owner gave them permission to use it, so long as they herded away the livestock before flying.

The most important thing the Wrights needed to address was the overly sensitive elevator of the 1903 design. The control response of the elevator was dampened in the subsequent airplanes by adding weight to the front to shift the center of gravity forward, and by mounting the elevator farther ahead of the wings. This reduced the tendency of the airplane to dart up and down and made it easier to fly. It was a slow process to rid the *Flyer* of its troublesome pitch problem, however. The Wrights did not match their 59-second 1903 effort until September 15, 1904, with the 49th flight of their second powered airplane. They made their first complete circle five days later. That flight lasted 1 minute 36 seconds and covered 4,080 feet.

The Wrights finally resolved the stability problems that had plagued them since Kitty Hawk in the fall of 1905, with their third powered airplane. Flights of several minutes were common now. On October 5, 1905, Wilbur made a spectacular flight in which he circled the field 30 times in 39 minutes for a total distance of 24.5 miles. By any measure, the 1905 *Flyer* was a practical flying machine. With it, the experimental phase of the Wright brothers' aeronautical work was brought to a close.

The Wright brothers were indeed the first to get an airplane off the ground, but the more important reason they are credited with the invention of the airplane is that they created a fundamentally new technology, one that could evolve and be developed to meet challenges unimaginable in 1903. Their inventiveness lies less in the hardware that carried them aloft on December 17, 1903, than in their comprehension of the essential barriers to mechanical flight and their design solutions to overcome them. The Wrights succeeded in inventing the airplane because they approached the problem with an effective methodology undergirded by innate skills, engineering techniques, and personality traits especially conducive to technical creativity. And therein lies the genius of Wilbur and Orville Wright.

IT IS NO PLEASANT THOUGHT TO US

THAT ANY FOREIGN COUNTRY

SHOULD TAKE FROM AMERICA ANY

SHARE OF THE GLORY OF HAVING

CONQUERED THE FLYING PROBLEM,

BUT WE FEEL THAT WE HAVE DONE

OUR FULL SHARE TOWARD MAKING

THIS AN AMERICAN INVENTION ...

Wilbur Wright 1905

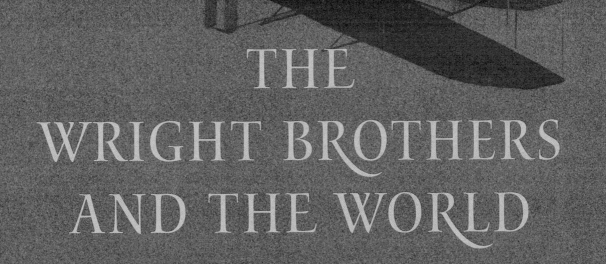

5

THE
WRIGHT BROTHERS
AND THE WORLD

Wilbur flies over a small but enthusiastic crowd at Le Mans, France, in August 1908—the first official public demonstration of their airplane.

WILBUR AND ORVILLE WRIGHT WOULD remember 1900-05 as their happiest years. The process of invention had given direction and purpose to their lives. In mastering an enormous challenge that had defeated all others, they had demonstrated their extraordinary talents and abilities and proved their courage. Orville expressed their sense of exhilaration in a letter to a friend: "Isn't it astonishing that all these secrets have been preserved for so many years just so that we could discover them!!"

And then it was over. By October 1905, the Wright brothers had a practical airplane in hand. Now they faced a new challenge. They would set the bicycle and printing businesses aside and devote all of their energies to selling their invention. It would be far more difficult than they had imagined.

The first potential customer arrived at their home on October 24, 1904. Brevet Lt. Col. John Edward Capper, Royal Engineers, a senior officer of the British military balloon establishment, was in America to visit the aeronautical exhibits and demonstrations that were part of the great Lewis and Clark Exposition then under way in St. Louis, Missouri. Before his departure from England, Capper had asked fellow members of the Royal Aeronautical Society (RAeS) whom he should meet while in America. By all means, he was told, he should pay a visit to the mysterious Wright brothers in Dayton, Ohio.

At the time, leading English aeronautical enthusiasts were familiar with the names of Wilbur and Orville Wright. Their claims to have flown at Kitty Hawk, North Carolina, in 1903 were generally known, although by no means universally believed. Patrick Alexander, an influential member of the RAeS, had met the brothers during a visit to America. B.F.S. Baden-Powell and a handful of others had corresponded with them. The Wrights had not communicated with any of their European contacts since 1903, however, and no one had the slightest idea what they had been up to since that time. Capper hoped to take their measure for himself.

As predicted, Dayton proved to be the most instructive stop on Capper's American tour. Although the Wrights did not show him their airplane, they did allow him to study photographs of their 1904 flights. Capper was impressed, and suggested that the Wrights offer their invention for sale to the British War Office. "We told him," Orville explained, "that we were not yet ready to talk business."

The success of the longer flights at the close of the 1904 flying season changed their minds. Recognizing that they would "be ashamed of ourselves" if they did not offer the U.S. government the first opportunity to purchase their invention, the brothers asked the advice of Dayton Congressman Robert M. Nevin, who promised to see that their offer was presented to the secretary of war.

The Wrights wrote to Colonel Capper on January 10, 1905, remarking that they were now prepared to offer the British government an airplane capable of carrying two men through the air at a speed of 30 miles per hour. Eight days later, the brothers sent yet another letter to Congressman Nevin, describing the performance of their machine and offering terms for its sale.

Nevin's office forwarded the letter directly to the U.S. Army Board of Ordnance and Fortification for comment. Maj. Gen. G. L. Gillispie, president of the board, replied on January 26, explaining that the U.S. government would not discuss the matter until such time as it was presented with a machine that had been "brought to the stage of practical operation without expense to the United States."

Wilbur and Orville were outraged. The Army obviously doubted their assurance that their machine was "fitted for practical use." The sons of Bishop Milton Wright had no intention of dealing with anyone who did not recognize them as honest men. "It is no pleasant thought to us that any foreign country should take from America any share of the glory of having conquered the flying problem," Wilbur wrote to Octave Chanute on June 1, "but we feel that we have done our full share toward making this an American invention, and if it is sent abroad for further development the responsibility does not rest upon us."

It is important to note that the War Department officials were not the shortsighted dullards that they appeared to be. The Army had rushed into the airplane business during the years 1898-1903, spending $50,000 on an unsuccessful aircraft designed by Samuel Pierpont Langley, third Secretary of the Smithsonian Institution. When that machine failed on two occasions in 1903, the U.S. Congress threatened to cut off all Army funds for aeronautical research and development. Small wonder that the same officers were reluctant to open negotiations with two "inventors" who claimed to have built an airplane in the back room of an Ohio bicycle shop.

The initial British reaction was more positive. Colonel Capper passed the Wright brothers' offer to his superiors with a covering note calling "very special attention" to the proposal. "I have every confidence in their uprightness," he remarked, "and in the correctness of their statements."

A War Ministry official wrote to the Wrights on February 11, 1905, inviting them to provide a description of the performance of their machine and a statement of terms. The brothers offered to provide an airplane carrying two men for a distance of between 10 and 50 miles at a speed of not less than 30 miles per hour for a price of £500 per mile covered during the first trial flight.

Intrigued, but daunted by the price, Richard Ruck, Capper's superior, passed the matter up the chain of command to the Royal Engineer Committee, the War Office body charged with making scientific and technical decisions. The committee suggested that the British military attaché in Washington be sent to Dayton to see the machine in the air before any decision was made.

Had a visit taken place in the spring of 1905, the Wrights might have been willing to allow an official English visitor the privilege of witnessing a flight. Unfortunately, the attaché was absent in Mexico, and did not make contact with the brothers until November 18, by which time the brothers' attitude toward the sale of their machine had changed. With the successful conclusion of the 1905 flying season, the Wrights knew that they had developed a practical flying machine.

They understood that the value of their machine lay not in the metal, wood, and fabric, but rather in the principles on which it was constructed and the solid information on which its design was based. Their invention would be difficult to protect from those who might try to copy it. The patent would not be granted until 1906. Premature disclosure of the details might destroy their legal position.

Even the patent would not provide a guarantee of protection. Other inventors, from Eli Whitney to Alexander Graham Bell had been forced to pursue in costly lawsuits those who infringed on their patents. The wisest course, they decided, was to reveal as little about the airplane as possible until they had a signed contract for its sale in hand. Until then, there would be no more flying.

Any attempt to explain the career of Wilbur and Orville Wright during the difficult years after 1905 must begin with an understanding of their basic assumptions about the world. Like their father, they saw the world as a very dangerous place for honest folk. The brothers fully expected that their moral fiber would be sorely tested, as had their father's, by mountebanks, charlatans, and thieves. That expectation shaped their approach to the business of selling their invention.

Octave Chanute, their closest and most trusted friend in the aeronautical community and an experienced businessman, urged them to fly their machine at once, before the largest crowd they could find. The impact of such a spectacle would bring instant fame, he argued, and force the governments of the world to come calling on them, hats in hand and purses open.

Wilbur and Orville refused to take that chance. Why should they exhibit their invention without legal protection, trusting that governments and individuals, inspired by a sense of justice and fair play, would repay them for their efforts? It seemed far more likely that an unscrupulous rival would copy their technology and undersell them, stealing both the money and the credit.

They would do business with the governments of the world on their own terms. The Wrights offered to provide a machine capable of meeting a set of mutually acceptable performance criteria, including a minimum speed, range, and carrying capacity. Once a contract was signed, the brothers would demonstrate their machine, fulfilling the terms of the agreement. No money would change hands until the customer was satisfied.

Wilbur and Orville thought it a perfectly fair arrangement that protected the interest of the buyer, while protecting their technology from rivals. Unfortunately this approach made bureaucrats, who were intent on not looking foolish, very nervous indeed. If these fellows from Dayton could fly, why did they not do so? If they had photographs of their machines in the air, why did they not show them? And what if they could not really fly at all? How would the contracting officer look then?

The Wright brothers set out in the fall of 1905, determined to sell the airplane in their own way. They wrote directly to Secretary of War William Howard Taft, complaining that their initial proposal had received "scant attention" from the Army. The brothers did not want to seek a buyer abroad, "unless we find it necessary to do so." Their initial offer stood. Ten days later, Orville made the same offer to the War Office in London.

The response from the United States War Department was swift and predictable. Maj. Gen. J. C. Bates, the new president of the Board of Ordnance and Fortification, informed them that the board would not consider the matter until the Wrights provided detailed drawings and descriptions of their machine, precisely what Wilbur and Orville would not do.

Wilbur asked what sort of performance the board would expect of a flying machine. Bates explained that the Army would not formulate requirements, or take any further action on the subject, "until a machine is produced which, by actual operation, is shown to be able to produce horizontal flight and to carry an operator." The word of two bicycle makers from Dayton was still not good enough.

The British response was more promising. The military attaché in Washington wrote to the brothers on November 18, 1905, asking when and where a British officer could see a Wright machine in the

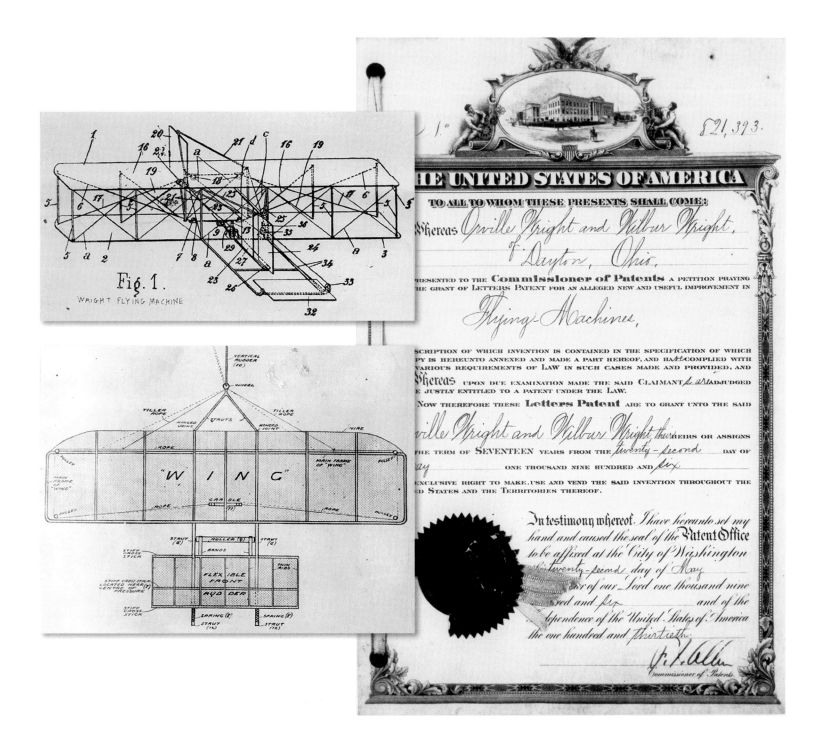

After several rejected applications, the Wright brothers finally achieved patent protection for "an alleged new and useful improvement in Flying-Machines." The detailed drawings at left accompanied a 1908 Wright patent application.

air. Wilbur replied that a demonstration flight was now out of the question, but offered to introduce the attaché to prominent local citizens who had seen them fly. Once a contract was signed, the Wrights would be more than happy to meet the terms agreed upon by flying their 1905 machine.

Embassy officials explained that they were not empowered to interrogate witnesses or negotiate contracts. Their instructions limited them to observing a flight and reporting back to London. The demonstration was a prerequisite for opening discussions, not something that would occur after the deal was closed. English officials like Capper knew that "the manufacture of a flying machine for scouting purposes has actually been effected." In view of their difficulty in dealing with the Wrights, however, even the most farsighted officers decided to drop negotiations with the Americans in favor of establishing a government-sponsored program of aeronautical research and development. What the Wrights had done, English engineers could do as well.

The Wright brothers now turned their attention to France. With the exception of Clément Ader, most French aeronautical enthusiasts had focused on lighter-than-air flight during the last decade of the old century. The Aéro-Club de France, founded in 1898, was the resort of one of the wealthiest and most fashionable social sets in fin de siècle Paris—the sport balloonists. By 1900, however, some leading members of the Aéro-Club had begun to transform the organization into something more than a sportsman's club. Henri Deutsch de la Meurthe, a pioneer of the French petroleum industry and an enthusiastic supporter of any vehicle powered by an internal combustion engine, led the way. In the fall of 1900, Deutsch de la Meurthe established a 100,000-franc prize for the first airship flight from the Aéro-Club's Parc d'Aérostation at Saint Cloud to the Eiffel Tower and back in half an hour or less.

After several abortive attempts, Alberto Santos-Dumont won the Deutsch Prize on October 19, 1901. In typically grand style, the wealthy young Brazilian donated 75,000 francs to the Paris poor and divided the remaining prize money among the members of his crew. In the wake of his Deutsch Prize victory, however, even Santos-Dumont lost his enthusiasm for the airship. "To propel a dirigible balloon through the air," he remarked, "is like pushing a candle through a brick wall."

Capt. Ferdinand Ferber, a serving officer and aeronautical experimenter, sensed that Aéro-Club enthusiasm for lighter-than-air flight was waning by 1902 and saw an opportunity to draw the organization into the mainstream of heavier-than-air developments. Ferber, who first learned of the work of the Wright brothers in 1901, had actually built and flown a "type de Wright" glider in 1902-03.

In February 1903, Ferber published an article in which he warned patriotic Frenchmen that the United States had taken leadership in aeronautics. He called for other enthusiasts to join him in gliding experiments that would enable France to recapture the lead from Langley, Chanute, and those mysterious figures, "Messrs. Orville and Wilbur Wright of Dayton, Ohio, USA."

Two months later, on the evening of April 2, 1903, Octave Chanute, who was visiting his native Paris on behalf of the committee planning the upcoming Lewis and Clark Exposition in St. Louis, Missouri, gave the most important speech of his life to members of the Aéro-Club de France. During the course of his address, Chanute described his own work and that of other American flying machine pioneers and closed with a description of the Wright experiments of 1900-02. The lecture fanned the spark kindled by Ferber's article into an open flame.

An aging widower who had returned in triumph to the city of his birth, Chanute exaggerated his own role and misrepresented his relationship with the Wrights. More important, he described the Wright technology in inaccurate terms. As a result, pioneer French experimenters began their work with some fundamental misunderstandings about Wright aircraft. In spite of its inaccuracies, Chanute's talk sent a shock reverberating through the French aeronautical community, convincing many that "les frères Wright" were well on their way to solving the problems of mechanical flight. Ernest Archdeacon, a wealthy lawyer with a reputation as one of the most daring balloonists in France, was particularly disturbed. "Will the homeland of the Montgolfier* [brothers]," he asked, "suffer the shame of allowing this ultimate discovery of aerial science … to be realized abroad?"

Recognizing an opportunity, Ferber wrote to Archdeacon, suggesting that a glider competition sponsored by the Aéro-Club would breathe new life into French aeronautics. The notion appealed to the sportsman in Archdeacon. "Our experience has taught us that racing leads to improved machines," he noted, "and the airplane must not be allowed to reach successful achievement in America."

At a meeting of the Aéro-Club Technical Committee on Aerial Locomotion on May 6, 1903, Archdeacon offered to contribute 3,000 francs to establish a prize fund for a glider competition. The members created a special Sub-committee on Aviation Experiments, with dirigible builder Charles Renard as president and Archdeacon as secretary. The competition was never held, but the Aéro-Club was soon the headquarters for "les aviateurs militantes," a band of determined experimenters, including Robert Esnault-Pelterie, Archdeacon, Gabriel Voisin, and others who built and tested copies of the Wright 1902 glider.

Based on inaccurate information and drawings supplied by Chanute and a complete misunderstanding of the nature of the Wright control system, these gliders were more than a bit disappointing. Still, they did serve as an entry point for a generation of the young pioneers who would bring France into the air age.

Wilbur wrote to Captain Ferber on October 9, 1905, providing him with a full account of their successes during the 1905 flying season and offering to discuss the sale of their flying machine to the

* The Montgolfier brothers were the first humans to fly in a lighter-than-air craft. They made a short flight in a hot-air balloon of their own construction near Paris on November 21, 1783.

1908: *With patents secured, the brothers set out to market their invention. Here Wilbur explains the machine's fine points to prospective buyers and onlookers in Le Mans during a sales trip to Europe.*

FOLLOWING PAGES | 1908: *Wilbur soars above the Hunaudières race course at Le Mans, a hundred miles from Paris. The week spent demonstrating flight at Le Mans earned the Wright brothers international renown.*

French government. Wilbur later communicated to him that the price would be one million francs (about $200,000). Ferber presented the letter to Colonel Bertrand, the officer in charge of balloon and airship research for the French Army, who agreed to recommend the appointment of a commission to investigate the Wright claims.

While awaiting Ferber's reply, the Wrights sent out three more accounts of the 1905 flights to contacts in England, France, and Germany. They hoped to stir the pot a bit, hurrying the French along, reawakening interest in England, and perhaps catching the attention of the Germans as well.

The publication of the letter in the French journal *L'Aerophile* created an immediate reaction in France. It was easy enough to pass off the best Wright flight of 1903 (852 feet in 59 seconds) as one step toward an as yet unrealized goal. The Wrights had been useful to enthusiasts like Ferber, Archdeacon, and Deutsch de la Meurthe, who could hold them up as a warning of the progress being made in America. The claims for the 1905 flying season were quite another matter, however. If the Wrights had actually covered distances of up to 25 miles on a single flight, then the game was over.

No member of the Aéro-Club de France was more fascinated by the Wrights than Frank S. Lahm. A native of Canton, Ohio, born in 1847, he had come to Paris in 1880 to sell Remington typewriters, and stayed to establish a company of his own. By 1905, he was a very wealthy man, and one of the most active sport balloonists in France.

Excited by the possibility that two fellow Ohioans had achieved success with a flying machine, he asked relatives and friends in the Dayton area to look into the matter. Having investigated the Wrights' story, and interviewed a number of witnesses who had seen them fly at Huffman Prairie, one of Lahm's contacts wired some startling news back to Paris on the evening of December 3, 1905: "Claims fully verified, particulars by mail."

Confirmation of that report arrived in Paris later that month. Intrigued by the Wrights' published letter, a reporter for *L'Auto* traveled to Dayton. He cabled the results of his independent investigation to his editor on December 12: "It is impossible to doubt the success of their experiments."

The first installment of a four-part story appeared in *L'Auto* on December 23, 1905. When the members of the Aviation Committee of the Aéro-Club met that evening, most regarded the account as a complete fabrication. A handful of others thought that there might be a kernel of truth in the Wright claims.

Frank Lahm presented the full report from his investigators in Dayton at a second meeting nine days later. Questions were shouted from the floor. If the Wrights had flown 25 miles, as reported, why was the story not headline news in America? Why did the Wright brothers not travel to France and capture the 50,000-franc prize for a circular flight of one kilometer recently established by Deutsch de la Meurthe and Archdeacon? Why was their own government not interested?